BUSINESS, MONEY, AND THE RISE OF CORPORATE PACs IN AMERICAN ELECTIONS

Recent Titles from Quorum Books

BUSINESS, MONEY, AND THE RISE OF CORPORATE PACs IN AMERICAN ELECTIONS

Theodore J. Eismeier
Philip H. Pollock III

Q

QUORUM BOOKS
New York • Westport, Connecticut • London

37.95

10-2-61

Library of Congress Cataloging-in-Publication Data

Eismeier, Theodore J.
  Business, money, and the rise of corporate PACs in
American elections.

  Bibliography: p.
  Includes index.
  1. Business and politics—United States.
2. Corporations—United States—Political activity.
3. Political action committees—United States.
4. Campaign funds—United States. I. Pollock,
Philip H. II. Title.
JK467.E47 1988   322'.3'0973   88-4054
ISBN 0-89930-322-6 (lib. bdg. : alk. paper)

British Library Cataloguing in Publication Data is available.

Library of Congress Catalog Card Number: 88-4054
ISBN: 0-89930-322-6

First published in 1988 by Quorum Books

Greenwood Press, Inc.
88 Post Road West, Westport, Connecticut 06881

Printed in the United States of America

The paper used in this book complies with the
Permanent Paper Standard issued by the National
Information Standards Organization (Z39.48-1984).

10 9 8 7 6 5 4 3 2 1

Contents

Figure and Tables

Acknowledgments

The authors wish to thank Hamilton College and the University of Central Florida for their financial support, the Federal Election Commission for its technical assistance, and Susan E. Beal for her secretarial assistance.

BUSINESS, MONEY, AND THE RISE OF CORPORATE PACs IN AMERICAN ELECTIONS

1

Business in American Politics

The last decade has witnessed profound changes in the economy of American national elections, changes that were largely unforeseen when Congress set out to tighten the regulations on campaign finance in the wake of Watergate. The most widely remarked of these changes has been the growth of a new breed of political organization, the political action committee, and the most spectacular growth has come in the PACs of business. These committees of corporations and trade associations now number almost 2,500 and in the 1986 election made direct contributions of $60 million to congressional candidates, more than twice as much as all the direct contributions and coordinated expenditures of both political parties.

Controversy surrounds this new political wherewithal. To its supporters the organized involvement of business in the financing of campaigns is a legitimate form of political expression and one element of a belated response by corporations to the visible hand of government.[1] To critics, however, neither money nor the modern corporation fits easily into democratic theory and vision, and their coincidence in political action committees represents an ominous conjunction of political and economic power.[2] This worry, which is manifest in the wave of proposed new regulations on campaign finances, is part of a broader concern in some quarters about corporate hegemony in American politics. Indeed, the increasing involvement of business in politics occurred even as the intellectual center of gravity of students of that relationship was shifting.[3] Once thought of as one of a number of contenders for power, business is now widely regarded as occupying a privileged position in American politics.

Both the specific debate about campaign finances and the broader controversy about the political position of business have thus far generated more heat than light. In part the problem has been one of evidence. Although there is a growing body of empirical research on the contours of PAC activity—who gives how much to whom with what effect—not much is known about the internal lives of this new breed of political organization. Moreover, the new attention to the corporation by political scientists has not as yet produced a rich stock of empirical knowledge about what business firms actually do in politics and why.

Yet the problem is also one of theory. One encounters in the literature on PACs a curious single-mindedness in the assumptions about these organizations and in the methodology for studying them. Political action committees, viewed exclusively as creatures of campaign finance reform, are almost always cast as underlaborers in related fields: as new resources for campaign strategies of candidates; as private instruments for the buying of political power and access; as culprits or symptoms in the demise of political parties. PACs, in short, have been typecast as bit players—always more interesting for how they affect other actors than as actors themselves in need of explanation.

To be sure, our understanding of PACs and campaign finance is shaped by apposite theories of interest groups and business-government relations. The borrowing, however, is implicit and selective and the borrowed body of theory inchoate. This is certainly the case for the welter of conflicting interpretations of business's role in politics and government, and even the more developed theories of interest groups and power in the United States have been described by one recent reviewer as "quite confused."[4] Clearly some intellectual brush-clearing is in order.

The present-day heirs of the Progressive movement—citizen lobbies like Common Cause, the media and political journalists like Elizabeth Drew, scholars including Amitai Etzioni and others—have to a large degree shaped public debate about money in politics. According to Austin Ranney a core belief of these Neo-Progressives is that "the great enemies of society are the big political machines, the business 'trusts' and the other special interests that try to advance their selfish goals at the public's expense by buying elections and corrupting public officials."[5] Thus for Drew in *Politics and Money* the questions and answers about campaign finance are obvious: "Why is all this money floating about? What do investors expect? At a minimum they expect access, but access is only the required entry ticket for getting something done."[6] In this way arguments about PACs and campaign finance in the 1980s echo the rhetoric of the 1907 Tillman Act, which first barred corporate campaign gifts.

Ironically, the realpolitik of the public choice school of economics also has much in common with the Progressive tradition. Like the market for anything else, the argument goes, the market for politicians is fathomable by the standard tools of economics.[7] Such is the reasoning of a number of recent efforts to build and test econometric models of legislative influence by PACs as well as the logic of collective political action by firms.[8] Although the methods of these studies are diverse and the findings about the political purchasing power of campaign contributions decidedly mixed, they share at least the presumption that simple models of interest maximization take us a long way toward understanding the demand and supply of political influence.

Yet neither the model of corrupt exchange embedded in Neo-Progressive interpretations of the PAC phenomenon nor its restatement by neoclassical economists as a model of rational venality offers a complete or even accurate account of the behavior of corporate PACs, for on important issues they have at times too much and at times too little to say. Market models of politics say too much if they claim that the behavior of businesses and politicians is easily explicable as wealth and vote maximization,[9] and the facts of campaign finance further belie such generalizations. On the supply side of political influence, incumbent politicians typically have such large and diverse campaign war chests that even the largest contributions are likely to have very limited purchase.[10] On the demand side there is a tendency in corporate PACs especially to spread contributions so widely—the average contribution of corporate PACs to House candidates is less than $1,000—as to raise questions about their legislative intent and effectiveness. Thus organizational forms and expressive ideologies may be as important as narrow calculations of political self-interest in shaping PAC strategies.[11]

Moreover, on the matter of how in particular cases self-interest shapes tactics, the emerging orthodoxy has far too little to say. After all, the tactical behavior of corporate PACs is strikingly diverse. In 1980, for example, almost a third of corporate PACs gave 80 percent or more of their budgets to Republicans, but one in five gave 60 percent or more to Democrats. In the same election one-fifth of these PACs gave 80 percent or more of their budgets to incumbents, but more than a quarter allocated 60 percent or more to challengers and open seats. Faced with this diversity, some have been inclined either to ignore it or simply to assume that all such behavior must serve some interest and so by definition fit an economic model of politics. Yet such ostrichlike tactics do little to advance the understanding of political action committees.

Although political science traces its lineage to the Progressives, its study of campaign finance has been framed by broader questions about the play of power in American political institutions. The long history of controversy about interest groups and theories of power in the United States defies easy description, but our purposes will be served simply by identifying the major competing claims. The pluralist perspective on power—or at least a caricature of it—is the foil for a good deal of recent American writing on interest groups. For pluralists, power was thought to be widely though not equally distributed; the public good was approximated as a by-product of vigorous struggle among competing groups, each pursuing its own narrow agenda. By this view, campaign money was one of the many resources that groups, including business, used in the competition.

The theory of interest group liberalism was born as a critique of this received wisdom.[12] In fact, the argument goes, many potential competitors for influence are not organized, so that the few who are organized on any particular domain of policy are able to capture legislative and executive authority to turn it to their benefit. Business interests, which by this view are no different from other groups, actively seek government regulation for their markets as a way both to control entry and to establish regularized contacts with public authority. Campaign contributions merely cement these bonds.

This critique quickly became the new conventional wisdom and has now spawned its own body of revisionist scholarship on interest groups. One theme of this scholarship is that the world of interest groups is a good deal more diverse and competitive than the images of "capture" and "subgovernments" suggest. Indeed, even as the theory of interest group liberalism was gaining cachet in political science, political entrepreneurs were creating an explosion of new lobbies that could scarcely be expected by the theory. A second theme is that, in part because of the diversity of their clientele groups, government agencies have substantially more autonomy and discretion than the theory of interest group liberalism implies.[13] The discovery of an autonomous state and a variety of countervailing groups to the more widely recognized groups of economic producers has recently led to the development of a theory of "triadic power," which in some respects has more in common with pluralist thought than with the theory of interest group liberalism.[14]

There are two common threads in these otherwise divergent views of American interest groups. First, for each of them influence tends to be a segmental process; groups use people, money, expertise, and other resources to seek influence over particular politicians and bureaucrats for particular ends of policy. Thus there is relatively little discussion in this literature either of grand issues of policy or of links among interest groups and between these groups and the political parties. Second, in none of these various accounts of interest groups does business play an extraordinary role. To be sure, business is regarded as important and in many particular cases most powerful. However, in all of these theories business interests are to be understood in the same terms as organized labor, professional associations, farmers, and other groups.[15]

On both of these matters recent theorizing about the corporation in American politics differs sharply from earlier work on interest groups in general. For Charles E. Lindblom and others the minutiae of public policy, where the diverse interests of business may not always carry the day, are relatively uninteresting. It is the grand issues of policy—the distribution of wealth and income, the prerogatives of capital, the sanctity of property—that are most interesting and revealing of the real power of business. A close look at such issues, the argument goes, shows both collective purpose and extraordinary power going far beyond that wielded in the normal tug and pull of interest group politics.

One element of this power is, of course, money, and recent accounts of the corporate PAC phenomenon have emphasized the importance of collective action rather than the narrow pursuit of advantage by particular firms. Former Federal Trade Commissioner Michael Pertschuck, in reviewing the dismantling of some of the regulatory apparatus he helped to create, argues that in the last decade "corporate individualism—the narrow pursuit of individual company goals—gave way to the new corporate collectivism."[16] Michael Useem makes the same point explicitly about campaign finance: "Corporate PACs add company rationality to business giving, but they add an element of classwide rationality as well."[17] That classwide rationality, some have suggested, is achieved through the financial links between business and the national parties.[18]

All of this serves as a useful counterpoint to what may have been an overemphasis on the microeconomy of influence and inattention to the possibility of a distinctive political role for business in American politics. Yet both the logic of the argument about corporate privilege as well as its reading of the historical record are matters of dispute.[19] Indeed, a closer look at that record reveals the complexity of business–government relations in the twentieth century and provides important clues for understanding the political action of business in the 1980s. This is not to say that there is any consensual interpretation of this history,[20] but the facts do warrant four specific observations about the place of business in American politics.

First, compared with the history of business-government relations in other industrialized democracies, the development of the modern corporation and the modern state in the United States is distinctive.[21] Unlike Europe and Japan, where the growth of the state occurred before the rise of business bureaucracies, the growth of government in the United States occurred well after the birth of corporate giants. As late as 1929, Alfred D. Chandler, Jr., points out, "the government's working force in Washington was still a good deal smaller than that at United States Steel, General Motors, or Standard Oil. Then the change began. By 1940 a million civilians worked for the federal government. By 1970, nearly three million did."[22] Moreover, the growth of American government came largely as a response to the concerns of small businessmen and others about the perceived threat of the large corporations.

One consequence of this uneven development has been an adversarial strain in business–government relations. Thus regulation has been the instrument of choice for government intervention, and its attendant rhetoric has emphasized the need to control the abuses of big business. For its part business in its rhetoric has tended to cast government as an interloper, irrelevant to the growth of the American economy and threatening to its achievements.[23] The persistence of expressed antagonism between business and government sets the experience of the United States apart from that of other nations.

A second observation is that the reaction of business to the growth of government has been far from monolithic. At one level, of course, is the visceral response against the waves of reform and regulation in this century. As articulated by such umbrella organizations as the National Association of Manufacturers and the Chamber of Commerce, this response has often been pointedly critical. From the beginning, however, businessmen adjusted to the social forces that were changing government's role and became actively involved in shaping the course of reform:

Rather than regarding every expansion of government as a threat to their autonomy and profits, an enlightened segment of the nation's industrial and financial leadership began to realize that government had a useful role to play in conserving natural resources, improving public health, curbing deceptive trade practices, reducing pollution, compensating workers for injury on the job, and assuring the public of safe products. This is the essence of the doctrine of "corporate liberalism."[24]

If government could play a useful role in promoting the commonweal, so too could it serve the interests of particular industries. The extent of business dominance of the regulatory process is a matter of continuing debate,[25] but it is clear that some industries came not only to accept but to welcome government intervention in their markets.

The diverse reactions of business to the rise of the positive state have in part been the product of cleavages within the business community. Regulated versus unregulated, region versus region, small versus large, exporters versus non-exporters—these and other divisions have created a lively pluralism in business politics, often pitting corporate interests against each other as much as other groups.[26] Yet even within industries and firms there has been a mix of motives. Indeed, active pursuit of government's largesse has often coexisted with an antigovernment ideology. Thus, demands for price guarantees, protection from foreign competition, barriers to entry, and other subventions by government have often been made by those who at the same time hail the virtues of laissez-faire. The tension between purism and pragmatism helps to define the distinctive character of business political action in the United States.

This character is also defined by a third feature of the political history of business. Money has for all of this century been a prominent part of corporate involvement in electoral politics, but the forms and beneficiaries of these contributions have changed. The political money of business was highly partisan at the turn of the century, and its financial links to the Republicans quite formal:

> [Mark] Hanna, in his capacity as Chairman of the RNC, levied regular assessments on businesses of consequence throughout the nation. No distinction was made between "big business" and "business." Assessments were apportioned according to each company's "stake in general prosperity" and to its special interest in a region. Banks, for example, were assessed one quarter of one percent of their capital; Standard Oil contributed about a quarter of a million dollars, and the large insurance companies slightly less. If a company sent in a check Hanna believed to be too small, it was returned. If a company paid too much, a refund was sent out.[27]

Reforms in campaign finance law and changing calculations of political self-interest by business and other groups have wrought a succession of changes in the way money flows into American national elections. The most obvious changes have been in the structure of donations. After the Tillman Act donations from business came not directly from the coffers of corporations but from the contributions—some very large—of their executives. Such individual contributions have in turn been increasingly regulated, and since the 1970s a growing share of them have been channeled through the corporate political action committee.

There have been changes as well in the beneficiaries of these contributions. At the turn of the century business aimed most of its money at the Republicans and most of its ire at the Democrats. As early as the 1920s, however, corporate executives had become somewhat more bipartisan in their giving and in their aggregate contributions to congressional elections have remained so.[28] At the same time congressional elections have themselves changed in important ways. Like other players, business donors have had to adapt to a campaign environment that in the last two decades has become more and more candidate centered. During this period the demands of political entrepreneurship and of the new technologies of campaigning increasingly have driven the economy of national elections.[29]

This leads to a final observation. In its efforts to organize for political action and to influence public policy, business has been subject to the vicissitudes of American politics in the same way as other groups. Lindblom and the view of corporate privilege notwithstanding, business groups have hardly been omnipotent on important issues of policy. Indeed, during the 1960s and 1970s, precisely when the idea of corporate dominance began to gain currency, business was suffering a string of political setbacks on a host of regulatory and other issues it deemed to be of great importance.[30] Neither has business been immune from a variety of internal and external forces affecting most political organizations. The history of business efforts to work collectively toward common ends, for example, is replete with the same difficulties as other groups.[31] Moreover, both the increase in group activity by business and the accompanying proliferation of corporate political action committees in the last decade are reflections of systemic changes.

This reading of the history of business politics in the United States leads us to offer a more complex model of corporate political activity than is common among students of campaign finance. To be sure, the pursuit of narrow self-interest through crude exchange may be part of this activity. But placing business in American electoral politics requires a broader field of vision. To begin with, there is the organizational dimension. The structures through which political interests are pursued have lives of their own, helping to mold both goals and tactics. This, we shall argue, is no less true for business interests than it is for others. We shall also show how the variegated history of business–government relations in the United States has helped determine organizational ideologies and how the pursuit of ideology and interest has been influenced by changes in the electoral environment.

In Chapter 2 we propose a model of the organization and political behavior of corporate interests. For this perspective we draw upon a rich resource—the hundreds of political action committees formed by corporations. The argument here is that only part of the story of business behavior is told by crude exchange; the rest is told by important but widely ignored organizational forces. Here we describe the play of a larger set of strategies pursued by PAC decision makers and show how these strategies are shaped by a set of organizational constraints.

Thus in Chapter 2 we argue that corporate PACs are best understood as groups whose behavior is influenced by ideological, structural, and environmental forces. In the next three chapters we expand and apply these ideas. The argument in Chapter 3—accommodationist business strategies—the effort to curry favor with the congressional powers that be—is shaped by organizational ideologies characteristic of PACs whose parent firms are the subjects of "old-style" economic regulation. Firms that perceive themselves as victims of "new-style" social regulation, by contrast, often develop organizational ideologies of opposition to government, and they may use their PACs as instruments of adversarialism and partisanship.

The distinction between old- and new-style regulation—economic and social regulation some have termed it—is not new. What we seek to do in Chapter 3 is to identify more clearly the political implications of the distinction and to match theory more closely with data. Building upon the arguments of this chapter and recalling the importance of organizational ideologies, discussed in Chapter 2, we specify which sectors of business are likely to favor accommodation and which are more prone to adopt strategies of opposition. These theoretical expectations are then tested against the record of campaign contributions of corporations in the 1980 and 1984 elections. Our basic resource is the data of the Federal Election Commission, which in this task we have enriched with additional information about the economic activity of parent firms.

Chapter 4 takes a closer look inside corporate PACs. Where are these PACs located? Do PACs nationalize campaign finance or are they tied to local and regional candidates? Do large organizations behave differently from small ones? Do PACs with highly developed national connections pursue different strategies than PACs located in the hinterland? Apposite scholarship in organization theory and campaign finance suggests interesting answers to these questions. After identifying the points of convergence and divergence in the literature, we turn again to the data about campaign spending, here enriched with information about organizational characteristics.

Chapter 5 turns from the factors that affect individual organizations independently of other groups and quite apart from the larger electoral setting to the role of outside agents in influencing the strategic choices of PACs. In this chapter we consider the role of outside forces in shaping the aggregate contours of corporate spending in 1980 and 1984. How important are networks among PACs and ties between PACs and parties in any given election? What may cause the apparent interelection variation in the overall distribution of business money?

Most corporate PACs are individually quite modest and, as a group, motivationally quite diverse, yet we shall show that there is an aggregate logic in their patterns of spending. In 1980, for example, the overall pattern reflected a pro-Republican tilt; in 1984 incumbents of both parties were the beneficiaries of PAC largesse. These data open the door for a discussion of the questions we have framed. In any given election we need to look at the effect of bellwether PACs, the demands of candidates, and the role of the national party organizations. Thus interelection differences in the distribution of campaign money reflect a change in the balance of these factors or a more general change in the climate of partisan expectations. In Chapter 5 we consider the changes that have occurred in the 1980s.

Of course, the organized involvement in American elections through political action committees is still in a process of development. Having shown how the behavior of this new breed of political organization is affected by a complex set of internal and external forces, we shall in the final chapter consider where their own evolution and the changing political environment will place them in American politics in the years ahead. Here we shall consider how various proposals to change once again the campaign finance laws would affect the PACs of business. A larger argument will be made about the continuing tension between pragmatism and ideology in the American business community. Republicans were the beneficiaries of the triumph of ideology in 1980; Democrats were able in 1984 and 1986 to block the flow of Republican venture capital by appeals to pragmatism. The future role of the political money of business, we argue, will depend both on the course of public policy and on the parrying of the national parties.

Notes

1. Bernadette A. Budde, "The Practical Role of Corporate PACs in the Political Process," *Arizona Law Review* 22, no. 2 (1980), pp. 555–68; Lee Ann Elliott, "Political Action Committees: Precincts of the 1980's," *Arizona Law Review* 22, no. 2 (1980), pp. 539–54.

2. Thomas B. Edsall, *The New Politics of Inequality* (New York: W. W. Norton and Co., 1984); Amitai Etzioni, *Capital Corruption* (New York: Harcourt Brace Jovanovich, 1984).

3. The seminal work is Charles E. Lindblom, *Politics and Markets* (New York: Basic Books, 1977). See also Thomas Dye, "Oligarchic Tendencies in National Policymaking: The Role of Private Policy-Planning Organizations," *Journal of Politics* 40, no. 2 (May 1978), pp. 309–31; Lawrence B. Joseph, "Corporate Political Power and Liberal Democratic Theory," *Polity* 15, no. 2 (Winter 1982), pp. 246–67; John Manley, "Neopluralism: A Class Analysis of Pluralism I and Pluralism II," *American Political Science Review* 77, no. 2 (June 1983), pp. 368–83; Sidney Plotkin, "Corporate Power and Political Resistance: The Case of the Energy Mobilization Board," *Polity* 18, no. 1 (Fall 1985), pp. 115–37; Kay Schlozman, "What Accent the Heavenly Chorus? Political Equality and the American Pressure System," *Journal of Politics* 46, no. 4 (November 1984), pp. 1006–32; Michael

Useem, *The Inner Circle* (Oxford: Oxford University Press, 1984). Critical reviews of this revisionism include Robert Hessen, ed., *Does Big Business Rule America?* (Washington, DC: Ethics and Public Policy Center, 1981); Robert H. Salisbury, "Business and Government in America: Ordinary Clout and Contingent Privilege," paper presented at the annual meeting of the Midwest Political Science Association, Chicago, April 18–20, 1985; David Vogel, "The Power of Business in America: A Reappraisal," *British Journal of Political Science* 13, no. 1 (January 1983), pp. 19–43; David Vogel, "The New Political Science of Corporate Power," *The Public Interest* 87 (Spring 1987), pp. 63–79.

4. Andrew S. McFarland, "Interest Groups and Theories of Power in America," *British Journal of Political Science* 17, no. 2 (April 1987), pp. 129–47.

5. Austin Ranney, *Channels of Power* (New York: Basic Books, 1983), p. 53. For an excellent account of how this core belief has influenced the media's converage of the issue of campaign finance, see Frank J. Sorauf, "Campaign Money and the Press: Three Soundings," *Political Science Quarterly* 102, no. 1 (Spring 1987) pp. 25–42.

6. Elizabeth Drew, *Politics and Money* (New York: Macmillan, 1983), p. 77.

7. The classic statement of this view is George Stigler, "The Theory of Economic Regulation," *Bell Journal of Economics and Management* 2, no. 1 (Spring 1971), pp. 1–21.

8. See, for example, Henry W. Chappell, Jr., "Campaign Contributions and Congressional Voting: A Simultaneous Probit-Tobit Model," *Review of Economics and Statistics* 64 (February 1982), pp. 77–83; Linda L. Johnson, "The Impact of Real Estate Political Action Committees on Congressional Voting and Elections," *AREUEA Journal* 11, no. 4 (Winter 1983), pp. 462–75; James B. Kau and Paul H. Rubin, *Congressmen, Constituents, and Contributors* (Boston: Martinus Nijhoff, 1982); Gregory M. Saltzman, "Congressional Voting on Labor Issues: The Role of PACs," *Industrial and Labor Relations Review* 40, no. 2 (January 1987), pp. 163–79; Jonathan I. Silberman and Gary C. Durden, "Determining Legislative Preferences on the Minimum Wage: An Economic Approach," *Journal of Political Economy* 84, no. 2 (April 1976), pp. 317–29; W. P. Welch, "Money and Votes: A Simultaneous Equation Model," *Public Choice* 36, no. 3 (1981), pp. 209–234.

9. James Q. Wilson, *The Politics of Regulation* (New York: Basic Books, 1980), pp. 358–63.

10. Michael J. Malbin, "Campaign Financing and the 'Special Interests,'" *The Public Interest* 56 (December 1979), pp. 21–42.

11. Theodore J. Eismeier and Philip H. Pollock III, "Political Action Committees: Varieties of Organization and Strategy," in Michael J. Malbin, ed., *Money and Politics in the United States* (Chatham, NJ: Chatham House, 1984), pp. 122–41; Edward Handler and John R. Mulkern, *Business in Politics: Campaign Strategies of Corporate Political Action Committees* (Lexington, MA: Lexington Books, 1982); Frank J. Sorauf, "Who's in Charge? Accountability in Political Action Committees," *Political Science Quarterly* 99, no. 4 (Winter 1984–85), pp. 591–614.

12. The most important statements of this position are Theodore J. Lowi, *The End of Liberalism* (New York: W. W. Norton and Co., 1969); Grant McConnell, *Private Power and American Democracy* (New York: Alfred A. Knopf, 1966). Their claims were buttressed by Mancur Olson, Jr., *The Logic of Collective Action* (Cambridge: Harvard University Press, 1965).

13. These are among the themes of James Q. Wilson's work in *The Politics of Regulation* as well as his *Political Organizations* (New York: Basic Books, 1973).

14. McFarland uses this term in "Interest Groups and Theories of Power in America,"

where he also suggests that "the older pluralist outlook of the 1960's might provide some basis for a theory of power, groups, and process in the 1980's."

15. On this point see Vogel, "The New Political Science of Corporate Power."

16. Michael Pertschuck, *The Revolt Against Regulation* (Berkeley: University of California Press, 1982), p. 59.

17. Michael Useem, *The Inner Circle*, p. 140.

18. See, for example, Edsall, *The New Politics of Inequality*, chs. 1–3.

19. See, for example, James Q. Wilson, "Democracy and the Corporation," in Hessen, ed., *Does Big Business Rule America?*, pp. 35–39; Vogel, "The Power of Business in America: A Reappraisal"; Vogel, "The New Political Science of Corporate Power."

20. See, for example, Edwin M. Epstein, *The Corporation in American Politics* (Englewood Cliffs, NJ: Prentice Hall, 1969); Louis Galambos, *The Public Image of Big Business in America, 1880–1940* (Baltimore, MD: The Johns Hopkins University Press, 1975); Arthur Selwyn Miller, *The Modern Corporate State* (Westport, CT: Greenwood Press, 1976); David Vogel, *National Styles of Regulation: Environmental Policy in Great Britain and the United States* (Ithaca, NY: Cornell University Press, 1986), ch. 6; James Weinstein, *The Corporate Ideal in the Liberal State: 1900–1918* (Boston: Beacon Press, 1968); Robert H. Wiebe, *The Search for Order* (New York: Hill and Wang, 1967); Robert H. Wiebe, *Businessmen and Reform* (Cambridge: Harvard University Press, 1962); Wilson, *The Politics of Regulation*.

21. We draw here on Alfred D. Chandler, Jr., "Government Versus Business: An American Phenomenon," in John T. Dunlop, ed., *Business and Public Policy* (Cambridge: Harvard University Press, 1980), pp. 1–11; Thomas K. McCaw, "Business and Government: Origins of the Adversary Relationship," *California Management Review* 26, no. 2 (Winter 1984), pp. 33–52. Stephen Skowronek, *Building a New American State* (Cambridge: Cambridge University Press, 1982); David Vogel, "Why Businessmen Distrust Their State: The Political Consciousness of American Corporate Executives," *British Journal of Political Science* 8, no. 1 (January 1978), pp. 45–78.

22. Chandler, "Government Versus Business: An American Phenomenon," p. 4.

23. Francis X. Sutton, Seymour E. Harris, Carl Kaysen, and James Tobin, *The American Business Creed* (Cambridge: Harvard University Press, 1956), ch. 9; Vogel, "Why Businessmen Distrust Their State: The Political Consciousness of American Corporate Executives."

24. Vogel, *National Styles of Regulation: Environmental Policy in Great Britain and the United States*, p. 236. See also Weinstein, *The Corporate Ideal in the Liberal State: 1900–1918*; Wiebe, *Businessmen and Reform*.

25. For example, compare Gabriel Kolko, *The Triumph of Conservatism* (Chicago: Quadrangle, 1967) with Wilson, *The Politics of Regulation*.

26. Raymond Bauer, Ithiel De Sola Pool, and Lewis Anthony Dexter, *American Business and Public Policy* (New York: Atherton Press, 1964); Epstein, *The Corporation in American Politics*, pp. 226–29; Salisbury, "Business and Government in America: Ordinary Clout and Contingent Privilege"; Wiebe, *Businessmen and Reform*, pp. 10–15; Vogel, "The New Political Science of the Corporation."

27. George Thayer, *Who Shakes the Money Tree?* (New York: Simon and Schuster, 1973), pp. 49–50. The Democratic party had a much smaller number of corporate supporters.

28. Louise Overacker, *Money in Elections* (New York: Macmillan, 1932); Michael J. Malbin, "Looking Back at the Future of Campaign Finance Reform: Interest Groups

and American Elections," in Michael J. Malbin, ed., *Money and Politics in the United States* (Chatham, NJ: Chatham House, 1984), pp. 232–76.

29. Edie N. Goldenberg and Michael W. Traugott, *Campaigning for Congress* (Washington, DC: Congressional Quarterly Press, 1984); Gary C. Jacobson, *The Politics of Congressional Elections* (Boston: Little, Brown, 1987).

30. Vogel, "The Power of Business in America: A Reappraisal"; Wilson, "Democracy and the Corporation."

31. Wilson, *Political Organizations*, ch. 8.

2

Corporate PACs in Organizational Perspective

As the number and putative importance of political action committees have grown, so too has scholarly attention to this new presence in electoral politics. Yet the attention has been uneven. Although much is now known about the general spending behavior of PACs, much less is known about their internal lives. Indeed, with a few prominent exceptions,[1] the empirical treatment of PACs is largely bereft of an appreciation of organizational dynamics. We find this somewhat curious since there is no convincing reason for regarding political action committees as things totally apart from political parties, interest groups, and the other associations that have long been objects of interest for students of political organizations.[2] Why not consider political action committees to be a new species of political organization? Why not think of their behavior as being shaped by their internal structures and resources and by the environments in which they operate?

The failure to ask such questions about PACs stems from an enduring bias in the study of interest groups. As we argued in Chapter 1, the parents of PACs, especially corporate parents, occupy an ambiguous status in conventional perspectives of interest representation, and so their PAC progeny too have been orphaned by group theory. Indeed, the architects of the most comprehensive survey of organized interests undertaken in the 1980s, a survey that has occasioned some rethinking of accepted notions about group strategies and maintenance, excluded "trade unions... business corporations... hundreds of nonprofit corporations, public interest law firms, university based research centres, independent commissions, newsletters, consulting firms, and the increasingly active national lobbying efforts of public agencies and state and local governments."[3] It is debatable whether, as Jack L. Walker suggests, the organizations on this list are distinct from conventional interest groups in that membership

in them "is not entirely voluntary, and their problems of organizational maintenance are entirely different."[4] However, it is beyond question that these exclu-
sions virtually define the centers of growth in interest representation. Over the
past decade or so many individual corporations have moved closer to the middle
of the political stage, perhaps augmenting or rechanneling their traditional affiliations. Thus despite the relative decline of trade associations, corporations alone
account for more than half of all organizations with a Washington presence.[5]
Conventional theories of groups, tethered to traditional forms of interest group
activity, do not tell us very much about this new corporate presence and thus
are unable to account for the behavior of corporate PACs.

Moreover, students of groups who have been alert to this altered organizational
landscape tend to draw too bold a line between the "old" group universe and the
"new" institutional setting. Robert H. Salisbury, for example, has importuned the
scholarly community to cast a wider net, to account for the role of "individual
corporations, state and local governments, universities, and most other *institutions* of the private sector" that "have come to dominate the processes of interest
representation in American national politics."[6] Yet he argues that corporations
and other "institutional interests" are so different from "member interest
groups" that one probably cannot find appropriate analogues in group theory—
such as the nature of member–leader relations or the role of group representatives—to describe them. Whereas the life of an interest group revolves around
attracting and holding members and establishing the legitimacy of its political
claims in the name of those who join, the interests of institutions "are politically
and analytically independent of the interests of particular institutional
members."[7] Institutions typically can expect longer lives, they enjoy more discre-
tionary resources, and they experience fewer problems of accountability.

It is not difficult to see why, given his broad distinction, Salisbury views the rise
of political action committees as merely a symptom, one of "Brobdingnagian
proportions,"[8] heralding the heightened political profile of institutions. And not
much good can come of any of this, for unlike the fragile yet pluralistic mix of
policy goals among interest groups, corporations and other institutions harbor a
conservative bias—a bias reflected well in the pragmatism of their political action
committees. "Corporate PACs," Salisbury claims, "continue to give significant
financial support to their supposed ideological enemies, liberal Democrats. Surely
this is a prime example of the pragmatism of institutions."[9] Thus the role of
ideology and purpose, the trade-offs of competing group strategies, the problems
of balancing national concerns with the parochial demands of local affiliates, the
political divisions among group elites—all the things that animate and give texture to the world of interest groups—tend to be denied the world of PACs.

Corporate PACs As Political Organizations

Of course, embedding the analysis of corporate political action committees in
apposite theory about formal associations requires, first of all, that we place

PACs in the appropriate organizational company. Though somewhat more than simply "money groups,"[10] most PACs need and get less commitment and participation from donors than do other organizations. In the case of corporate PACs, as with all parented committees, this is a consequence of federal law. Although a corporation is barred from contributing its funds to candidates, it may assume any of its PAC's administrative "overhead" expenses. Office space, staff salaries, phone costs, and all other lines in the operating budget are accounted separately from the amounts raised and allocated to candidates. A corporate political action committee, then, has two benefactors: a parent, responsible for its creation and much of its internal structure; and donors, without whose pooled support the PAC would have no external life. In the status of their donors corporate committees are, to use James Q. Wilson's familiar terminology, *caucus* organizations, not *primary* groups:

> There are, broadly speaking, two major kinds of voluntary association structures—the "caucus" form and the "primary" form. By "caucus" is meant an organization in which one or a few leaders carry out the work of the organization, supported by funds or other kinds of support contributed by persons who rarely, if at all, are brought together in meetings or are otherwise asked to concert their actions in cooperative ventures. A "primary" organization is one in which, whatever the role of officers, members regularly come together to act in concert and to discuss associational affairs or are otherwise mobilized to carry on group activities. ... A caucus organization has *contributors*, a primary organization has *members*.[11]

PACs share this caucus form with many other associations—notably public interest lobbies—in which there are few if any opportunities for meaningful face-to-face interaction between contributors.[12] And in the importance of their corporate sponsors PACs are not unlike the hundreds of other groups founded by and vitally dependent upon institutional patrons.[13] These basic organizational arrangements—low donor engagement, dependence on institutional sponsorship—place corporate PACs in the increasingly crowded company of pure staff groups.[14]

Staff groups, of course, are bound to behave differently from associations that rely on large memberships for survival. As ideal types, the staff organization and the pure membership group demonstrate contrasting versions of internal democracy. Relatively free from problems of maintenance, and occupying positions at the center of a potentially large pool of donations, leaders of many staff organizations are well insulated from contributor demands. To be sure, in the decisions they make, PAC officials on the whole feel constrained by their perceptions of what contributors *expect* the group to do.[15] And Frank J. Sorauf argues that there is a natural resonance between the concerns of donors, PAC officials, and the parent company—a harmony that fosters a "virtual representation" of contributor interests.[16] Still, in their formal trappings corporate committees probably conform about as closely to a democratic mold as their public interest brethren.[17]

One possible source of contributor influence—an elected board of directors—does not even exist for most staff organizations, but one may be established to help legitimize the actions of the group or to fulfill some ritualistic purposes. Though election law requires only the naming of a chairman and treasurer, most corporate committees are formally controlled by boards of "nonspecialist amateurs," company executives whose "service on the PAC is peripheral or perhaps entirely unrelated to their ordinary round of executive duties."[18] Virtually without exception, these boards are appointed by the firm's chief executive officer—not elected by PAC donors—and board makeup faithfully reflects the company's administrative, geographical, and functional divisions.[19] There is one interesting exception to this designed representativeness: Most corporate PAC boards have no stockholder representation.[20] This omission is probably less crucial than it may appear, since most corporate PACs do not solicit shareholders anyway. More important, in making its allocation decisions the typical board, regardless of its composition, merely endorses the recommendations of the corporation's political specialist. This specialist, usually the firm's vice-president for public affairs, often chairs the PAC:

> The most prevalent committee situation by far is the one in which the committee consists of a mix of nonspecialist amateurs and public-affairs specialists or where the latter, without actual membership, provide briefings and candidate recommendations. By rough estimate... it appears that in about three out of five cases the specialists are the major influence or the dominant factor in candidate selection.... Although the committee has the final say and may require good justifications, it will rarely reject, or even alter, recommendations.[21]

Edward Handler and John R. Mulkern's "rough estimate" might even underestimate the influence of the committee's professional, specialist staff.[22] Hence, were we to encounter a corporate PAC that was an exemplary model of the pure staff genre, we could be fairly certain that its internal life would not be plagued by policy indecision or factional squabbling. And it would probably show greater flexibility and adaptability than would a pure membership group.[23]

This idealization, however, provides us with only a first approximation, for within the real universe of corporate PACs there is a multitude of internal worlds and decision-making methods.[24] For one thing, many corporate committees empower large, multitiered, more vigilant governing boards who may wish to accommodate incumbents representing each of the firm's plant locations. Some, displaying what Edwin M. Epstein calls the "Frawley, Dart, or Ford phenomenon,"[25] become personalized vehicles of ideological expression for the company's chief executive. Still many others may have but a single staffer who, when it comes to deciding how to spend the PAC's money, is armed solely with the latest recommendations from the Republican National Committee. Obviously, to say that corporate committees as a class are staff-oriented groups is to say too little about them. What organizational resources—and constraints— help determine the strategies available to PAC decision makers?

Size and Centralization

We begin with a variable that, as we shall see, clearly differentiates the basic profiles of corporate PACs—budget size. All else being equal, will the strategic decisions of a PAC staff charged with allocating large sums of money differ from the decisions of those with less to spend? A large contribution budget, of course, signals a condition of abundance, and such "organizational slack" is an important catalyst for organizational change.[26] At a minimum we would expect resource-rich PACs to be more varied in their behavior than smaller operations having only enough funds to meet basic goals. Moreover, if big budgets bring venture capital, there may be a certain pattern to this diversification. To the extent that backing the candidacies of nonincumbents qualifies as innovative behavior, contributions from large committees would be more prone to end up with outsiders.[27]

Even so, a big budget usually carries some organizational baggage that may mitigate the tendency to "develop new purposes and activities chiefly to satisfy staff persons with particular concerns and values."[28] After all, as resources grow so do staffs and, more important, so do staff professionalization and political sophistication. For PACs this may mean the tempering of innovation with a more pragmatic attention to the protection of corporate economic interests. What is more, if increased financial wherewithal heightens the desire to establish a national presence, then a more risk-averse posture almost certainly will be the result. Washington-based staffs, who frequently work closely with the group's lobbying arm, will be more conversant with the arcane aspects of pending legislation, more immersed in the insular world of capital politics, and more attentive to the advantages of dealing with current officeholders.[29] Again, political action committees are not uniquely susceptible to such Potomac-borne afflictions. Michael T. Hayes points out that for most staff groups with stable resource bases, such as organizationally mature public interest lobbies, "[a]ccess has become increasingly important as symbiotic relationships are cultivated with sympathetic legislators, administrators, and reporters."[30] In sum, as we search for patterns in corporate PAC behavior we can be fairly sure of this: Washington committees, for reasons incidental to their size, will be pulled toward strategies of access.

Quite apart from the effects of a Washington location, or perhaps subsuming those effects, are the consequences of the staff group's basic structural form— federated or unitary. Indeed, David B. Truman considers this "the most useful distinction that can be applied to political organizations in the United States,"[31] and his rich analysis of its importance is familiar to students of group theory. Federation is, in short, a precarious arrangement: "The fundamental reason for the tendency toward disunity in federated organizations is not obscure, although its ramifications may be highly complex. By acknowledging in formal terms certain spheres of local or constituent autonomy, a federated organization establishes and, as it were, sanctifies subcenters of power."[32] Furthermore, this basic inclination toward disunity is made worse if the subunits antedate the central authority, or if the federation must meet some new threat that transcends local concerns. Truman sees some fascinating subtleties in this distinction. His argument that geographic federations are inherently more stable than those following functional lines is especially interesting:

> Though potential cleavages of major importance within a group may exist along geographic lines ... organization according to function especially tends to encourage interaction growing out of specialized subinterests. Because leadership at the lower levels of the structure is necessarily caught up in these subinterests, the problem of reconciling these potentially conflicting elements is delayed until it reaches the middle or top levels of leadership. ... On the other hand, the nonfunctional, or geographical, basis of organization tends to settle the task of adjusting conflicting subinterests upon the entire leadership at all levels by emphasizing interaction based on more inclusive shared attitudes.[33]

Perhaps Truman neglects one obvious advantage of federations—they are natural conduits for collecting financial resources—but his analysis does suggest some clear patterns. The staffs of federated PACs will allocate money in ways that suggest localism and they will be slower to respond to changes in the political environment; unitary PACs will be more mobile and less varied in their spending. And the tendency toward parochialism and immobilism will be more noticeable for PACs whose parents are engaged in a wide range of economic activity.[34]

It would appear that financial strength and its various correlates may add up to something of a mixed blessing for the leaders of large staff groups. In fact, the same forces that typically bring organizational abundance also foster conditions that intrude upon a staff's insularity and inhibit its discretion. In his analysis of the giants within the ranks of trade and membership PACs, John R. Wright finds that, contrary to received wisdom, "allocations are dominated by local inputs—recommendations of active members of the PACs at the state, congressional district, and county levels."[35] Thus the PAC manager who takes full fund-raising advantage of his organizational structure, perhaps in the hope of making the most of a strategy of access, can fall prey to his own success, since "the organizational arrangement *most* conducive to raising money ... is also the organizational arrangement *least* conducive to influencing congressional voting."[36]

The Importance of Ideas

The structural aspect of organizations has enjoyed a prominent position in the study of groups. One reason for this is that the basic way a group is set up often has happy if unintended results. For example, disunity and immobilism may be, in Truman's words, "the diseases of federation,"[37] but federated arrangements tend also to foster organizational democracy by providing forums for the expression and channeling of demands by competing factions.[38] Clearly, one can draw links between these traditional notions about organizational structure and the behavior of political action committees. There is another, more difficult parallel we wish to draw between group theory and corporate committees—the importance of ideology.

Indeed, in trying to explain the formation of groups, scholars have come to rely heavily on the role of purposive or expressive rewards. It was Mancur Olson, Jr., of course, who initially questioned the assumption for which Truman is remembered—that like-minded individuals would naturally form groups to protect or promote their shared interests.[39] According to Olson, people must receive more durable and divisible incentives, such as highly valued material inducements, which are not equally available to all potential groups. These selective incentives, of course, need not bear any substantive relation whatever to the collective purposes group elites may wish to pursue. But without them no one will join. Thus for Olson group formalization is at best problematic and in most cases dependent on rewards that are differentially distributed in society.

Paradoxically, Olson's theory achieved widespread acceptance just as a Trumanesque "wave" of group proliferation was apparently taking place. How can we reconcile this phenomenon with Olson's convincing theoretical account? This question has occasioned a variety of theoretical constructions, the best known of which is the notion of the political entrepreneur.[40] A political entrepreneur is a person who is driven by ardent ideological or moralistic convictions and is "willing to forego monetary gratifications entirely or defer them indefinitely" in the interests of establishing an ongoing organization.[41] Armed with considerable charisma or persuasive skills, the entrepreneur becomes the heart of a cadre of leaders who give life to the group. Of course, in order to survive most groups must eventually find more enduring organizational bases. But historically the entrepreneurial impulse has been an essential condition for the mobilization of groups that have had to surmount formidable barriers to collective action.

Yet the evidence suggests as well that entrepreneurialism may be a strategy in the formation of groups facing a variety of initial circumstances, including staff organizations that rely for formation on the benefactions of patrons. Indeed, Walker shows that individual ideological commitment and the willingness to gamble can be a creative admixture: "It requires boldness to provide start-up funds to an untested political entrepreneur or to patronize a cause that might create controversy. My data demonstrate that among all the patrons studied, private individuals are the most likely to provide backing for new organizational ventures, far out-distancing foundations and government agencies in their willingness to take risks."[42] We know that some PAC officials profess rather unexciting reasons for starting their PACs—as a way to gain visibility for their corporation; as a status requirement in keeping up with what other firms are doing; as a convenient "I gave at the office" deflection for the solicitations of candidates.[43] But the more prevalent justifications are either unambiguously ideological or betray ideological awareness tempered by a more pragmatic view of the political world. As one corporate PAC manager put it, "We were set up because management had a strong belief that business has a right and obligation to change the direction of government—and we started when they didn't like the direction of government."[44] Handler and Mulkern, who divide their sample of corporate committees into "pragmatic PACs" and "ideological PACs," find some intense differences of opinion between these two camps. The managers of many ideological PACs take issue both with government's straying from the true way of free enterprise and with the tactics of their pragmatic PAC counterparts:

> Some of the criticisms aimed at those who follow the pragmatic path convey strong personal feelings. PACs engaged in split giving [the practice of supporting more than one candidate in the same race] show, according to one respondent, "a complete lack of integrity." The same holds true for those who give indiscriminately to incumbents with antibusiness voting records. These PACs are "locked into a selfish pursuit of access," even though such a policy redounds to the detriment of the business community. "Access," observed an ideological critic, "can mean access to a turkey." PACs that underwrite liberal Democrats, warned another, "are feeding the alligators." A third used stronger language: "The bastards are contributing to the enemies of business."[45]

Now it is unclear just how widespread such sentiments are. But these ideological divisions will almost certainly have noticeable contributory effects, quite apart from other organizational differences between PACs.

And we would add to this specific ideological polarization the general tendency for most organizations, regardless of the circumstances of their creation, to develop ideological interpretations for their behavior.[46] In fact, the use of ideological explanations is pervasive. Even most of Handler and Mulkern's pragmatists—managers who prefer to give priority to corporate legislative interests—bristled at suggestions that they were not worthy defenders of free enterprise, or that they had abandoned the ongoing battle with organized labor.[47] Thus the difference between corporate PACs is not that some develop ideological justifications and others do not. The difference rather is that some behave in ways that suggest ideological direction, while others may use ideological language to promote the PAC to potential donors. Indeed, business associations generally have relied more heavily on ideological appeals than have other economic groups.[48] And although there is conflicting theory and evidence on this point, the frequent reference to collective purpose in PAC solicitation material perhaps reflects a basic organizational reality: Corporate PAC donors are reputedly more conservative—and certainly more Republican—than are the strategies of PAC leaders who pursue a pragmatic, legislative course.[49]

There seems to be ample justification for keeping our analysis open to the importance of ideology in shaping the renewed corporate involvement in politics. To be sure, legal reform is the proximate cause for the numerical growth of political action committees. But the initial decision to take advantage of the laws, and the ongoing decisions about what purposes the PAC is to serve, may be animated by a number of concerns, including corporate ideologies. We regard the ideological response of business to the newer regulatory environment as essential to an understanding of corporate PAC behavior, and we devote the next chapter to an exploration of it.

Outside Forces

Above all else, organizations seek to survive.[50] Less obvious are the reasons why some groups survive and others do not or, to put a finer point on it, why some organizations remain vigorous and unassailable while others, though staying "alive," lurch from one crisis to the next, perpetually on the brink of extinction.

Underlying this gradient are two organizational dimensions. First, according to Wilson, is the group's level of autonomy—"a distinctive area of competence, a clearly demarcated and exclusively served clientele or membership, and undisputed jurisdiction over a function, service, goal or cause."[51] An organization may thus be engaged in a constant struggle, not only with *opponents* (groups with mutually exclusive goals and memberships), but with an army of *competitors* (groups that share stated aims and prospective members). Competition shapes an organization's behavior in various ways. It may use marketlike tactics to lure supporters, touting the extra value of the selective incentives it offers. It may attempt to broaden its base by appealing to individuals who are not directly affected by the goals the group seeks. Or it may resort to extravagant claims of influence or effectiveness in achieving its aims. Among political action committees these strategems are quite typical of "nonconnected" PACs.[52]

Indeed for all parented committees, autonomy, at least with regard to prospective contributors, is not a serious problem. Of course, to the extent that a corporate PAC competes with others for the sympathies of the same incumbent or for the future loyalty of the same challenger, it may try to distinguish itself, perhaps by tailoring the size and timing of its contributions in an attempt to appear especially pivotal.[53] And some committees may suffer from membership problems that stem from exits by politically disgruntled executives.[54] A few of the larger PACs in fact confer highly visible recognition upon especially generous or faithful donors.[55] By and large, though, Sorauf is right: Since corporate PACs enjoy a monopoly over potential contributors, maintenance considerations do not normally turn on the competitive scramble to provide highly valued incentives.[56]

The interorganizational relations of corporate PACs are shaped less by differences in membership autonomy than by the consequences flowing from a second but related determinant of organizational survival, the sheer level of *resources* in the group's possession:

> [A]ssociations [must] be able to lay claim to a more or less stable supply of resources—members, money, issues, causes, and privileged access to governmental or other relevant institutions. In principle, many associations would like to obtain as much of these resources as possible—if not more members, then at least more money and better issues. In practice, the availability of these resources is limited by the number of prospective contributors and their preferences and by the existence of rival organizational claimants.[57]

In fact corporate political action committees vary widely in the resources they control. Budget size, which we have already discussed, is an obvious example, and later in this chapter we will describe the contours of this variable. Still, resources involve other things not so easily measured in dollars. Some committees came into existence early on in the PAC "explosion" and so are thought to possess a certain competence or to enjoy special passage into partisan circles. Others may compensate for their own paltry budgets by acting as middlemen between cash-rich but information-poor PACs and needy or solicitous candidates. For still others inter-PAC communication becomes a goal in itself, and they may want to affect the choices of other committees by shading the information they provide. Indeed, for present purposes it is convenient to divide the PAC world into two strata—an "upper" stratum of the relatively few organizations that command more of the scarce resources of money, information, or access, and a much larger "lower" stratum of committees seeking to survive in a more spartan environment. Of course this is a simplification. But it does have some interesting consequences for the behavior of corporate PACs.

First, it is widely believed that the recommendations of a few prominent committees bear directly on the decisions of PAC managers having compatible partisan or ideological inclinations. These "bellwether PACs" are the huge Washington-based operations with reputations as savvy political insiders or ideological opinion leaders. The committees most frequently anointed by seasoned observers as wielding such influence over corporate PACs are themselves not housed in corporations but rather are established by trade or membership associations. And their resources dwarf all but the very largest corporate PACs. The best known of the breed is the Business Industry Political Action Committee, which boasts an impressive contributions budget, a nationwide organization, and a communications network that supports a wide range of politicizing activities. BIPAC was created by the National Association of Manufacturers, and so its involvements—finding attractive challengers, providing seed money in primaries, and generally reading the partisan tea leaves—reflect the strongly pro-business ideology of its parent.[58] This bellwether's high-profile tactics and recommendations doubtless are familiar to the managers of all corporate PACs, and apparently even are resented by some.[59] The point is that BIPAC, along with perhaps no more than "half dozen major groups"[60]—the PAC established by the Chamber of Commerce is another example—may be influential enough to lend coherence to the individual decisions of the hundreds of corporate PACs whose relative lack of resources makes them open to suggestion.

Such suggestion or direction sometimes comes from a second source—the national party organizations. Of course if money were the only metric for gauging resources, the parties would finish each election cycle a distant second to the aggregate power of PACs.[61] Indeed in much of the literature parties are portrayed as unworthy competitors of political action committees, frequently outmuscled by these well-heeled upstarts.[62] In fact, the parties have become influential contenders among our upper stratum of resource-rich organizations, for they control information and possess political skills that help them to direct the flow of campaign dollars. Of course among corporate PACs it is information supplied by the Republican party that is generally more sedulously sought and provided. However, following their 1980 debacle the Democratic party, specifically Democratic Congressional Campaign Committee Chairman Tony Coelho, apparently decided to exploit the organization's special political resources more fully. Coelho's tactics are legendary: Cajoling, imploring—even thinly veiled threats—have all been brought to bear on those who control the campaign coffers of corporate committees.[63] Again, the success of such overtures is likely to depend not only on a committee's partisan predispositions, but also on the configuration of the other elements that affect its behavior. Yet to the degree that party elites can control vital information about upcoming campaigns, they can have an important impact on the channeling of corporate PAC dollars.

There is a third, less explicit way that the decisions and expectations formed within the upper stratum of organizations can broadly affect the allocations of their more modestly endowed counterparts. As with the appeals of the party committees, this outside force also is partisan in nature. But unlike the specific recommendations about particular races and candidates, this factor is a good deal less concrete, as the term we will use for it—"climate of partisan expectations"—implies. First identified as theoretically important by Gary C. Jacobson and Samuel J. Kernell, the role of partisan prophecy in accounting for the aggregate deployment of political capital is now widely acknowledged.[64] The Jacobson and Kernell model is based on an elegant handful of assumptions, chief of which is the plausible notion that campaign contributors prefer, all else being equal, to put their money into contests expected to be close. Thus in election years proclaimed by pundits to be auspicious for Republicans, campaign dollars will flow to Republican challengers (whose chances for victory are fortuitously enhanced) and to Democratic incumbents (who are perceived to be at risk). If the political grapevine counsels investors to anticipate a pro-Democratic climate, the symmetry changes: Republicans will "circle the wagons" in defense of reputedly endangered incumbents; Democrats will go on the offensive, seeking to install new officeholders in their places.

One can see that the outside influences on PAC behavior are not independent of one another, and clearly they will not always pull in the same direction. For example, bellwether committees or party elites may deliberately try to foster self-serving expectations, or they may rail strenuously and perhaps successfully against the prevailing partisan wind. And there is yet another set of actors that needs to be added to this chorus of outside voices—the candidates themselves, especially incumbents. It is a standard observation, frequently offered in the spirit of an indictment, that an inordinate amount of PAC money goes to incumbents of both parties.[65] To be sure, at least some of this tilt toward incumbents is the product of the simple PAC pragmatism. But there are important demand side effects as well, for incumbents can raise as much money as they think they will need to discourage would-be opponents.[66] Such strategic behavior by incumbents can have palpable effects. There is some evidence, for example, that early and substantial fundraising by Democratic incumbents in the 1983–1984 election cycle helped to modulate the generally pro-Republican electoral climate.[67]

Varieties of Corporate PAC Behavior

Corporate committees, we have argued, are not structurally unique. Rather, they are subject to many of the same forces that help define the lives of all groups, particularly the increasingly numerous breed of staff organizations. And given the possible variation across PACs in the dimensions we have identified—size, centralization, the role of ideology, the impact of partisan appeals—one would expect a corresponding diversity in the way corporate PACs behave. Such an expectation, of course, runs counter to received wisdom about political action committees. Indeed the widely held presumption—that corporate PACs are best understood as new instruments of institutional access and political influence—often leads scholars and critics to make empirical claims about PACs that, at a minimum, portray them as predictable and one-dimensional:

> PAC contributions have a legislative purpose. They are generally made by interest groups that have specific legislative goals and conduct organized Washington lobbying programs. In addition, they have a special "investment" quality and heavily favor incumbents over challengers, substantially adding to the imbalance in political financing between incumbents and challengers.[68]

Portrayals such as this are to be taken seriously, for in suggesting that most committees act the same way they also imply that any organizational differences we might find between PACs are truly irrelevant. To borrow Edwin M. Epstein's medical metaphor, if in their gross anatomy (general spending behavior) political action committees are much the same, then questions about their internal anatomy and physiology (size, ideology, and organizational structure) are uninteresting.[69]

A Profile of Corporate PACs

But the behavior of PACs, as it turns out, is really quite diverse. In Table 2.1 we present some basic information about them—their size, the number of candi-

Table 2.1
Profiles of Corporate PACs in 1980 and 1984:
Total Contributions, Number of Recipients, and Average Contribution

	Total Direct Contributions							
From $ To $	0- 2499	2500- 4999	5000- 7499	7500- 9999	10000- 14999	15000- 19999	20000- Over	Totals
1980 % (N)	33.5 (358)	18.4 (197)	10.3 (110)	6.1 (65)	9.3 (99)	5.6 (60)	16.8 (180)	100.0% 1069
1984 % (N)	31.2 (458)	15.9 (233)	8.7 (128)	6.8 (100)	9.1 (133)	6.0 (88)	22.3 (328)	100.0% 1468

	Total Number of Recipients							
Number	5	6-10	11-20	21-30	31-40	41-50	51-Over	Totals*
1980 % (N)	30.0 (321)	18.9 (202)	15.6 (167)	8.9 (95)	5.7 (61)	4.9 (52)	16.0 (171)	100.0% 1069
1984 % (N)	34.5 (506)	17.3 (254)	13.4 (197)	8.9 (130)	6.1 (89)	4.9 (72)	15.0 (220)	100.1% 1468

	Average Contribution							
From $ To $	0- 249	250- 499	500- 749	750- 999	1000- 1249	1250- 1499	1500- Over	Totals*
1980 % (N)	25.2 (269)	44.5 (476)	18.6 (199)	6.3 (67)	2.9 (31)	.9 (10)	1.6 (17)	100.0% 1069
1984 % (N)	11.9 (174)	40.1 (589)	25.8 (378)	11.8 (173)	3.7 (54)	2.4 (35)	4.4 (65)	100.1% 1468

*Row percents may not sum to 100% due to rounding error.

dates they support, and their average contribution.[70] These numbers paint a varied picture, and so we are at some risk in trying to describe the "average" committee. Even so, we can see that corporate PACs on the whole are not particularly well-heeled operations. About one committee in three had a House contribution budget of less than $2,500 in each year, and roughly half spent less than $5 thousand. Although corporate PACs are undeniably formidable as a class—they channeled some $12 million into House campaigns in 1980 and twice that amount in 1984—the figures in Table 2.1 make one wonder if *individual* donations are all but undetectable in a typical candidate's war chest. In each election year about one-third of all committees gave to the mandated minimum of five candidates, and about half supported ten or fewer. And, although PACs are permitted by law to contribute larger sums, in 1984 better than half of them—over two-thirds in 1980—gave modest average contributions of under $500. These numbers suggest that, if we were randomly to choose a corporate PAC for closer scrutiny, our selection probably would not turn out to be an organizational leviathan that routinely awards the legal maximum to a lengthy list of recipients. Furthermore, it almost surely would not enjoy an "insider's" location in the nation's capital. Though not reported in Table 2.1, our data show that thirty-one (2.9 percent) of the corporate PACs that were active in the 1970–1980 cycle boasted a Washington headquarters, a number that rose to only fifty-four (3.7 percent) four years later.

Still, corporate PACs are so varied that the data in Table 2.1 also support those who look for giants instead of dwarfs. After all, about one organization in five spent fairly robust amounts of $20 thousand or more; one in four contributed money to over thirty candidates; and, in 1984 anyway, one in five maintained a quite detectable average per-candidate allotment of at least $750. And if we add to our "Washington-based" group those committees located in Maryland or Virginia, the number of corporate PACs with this vantage point on national politics increases noticeably.[71]

The diversity of corporate committees is further demonstrated by looking at the sorts of candidates they favor with their largesse. Table 2.2 shows how corporate PACs distributed their support across four types of House recipients in 1980 and 1984: Democratic incumbents, Republican incumbents, Democratic nonincumbents, and Republican nonincumbents. Again, the habitual pattern of the typical committee is not to be found here. Indeed, these organizations seem unified only in their unwillingness to support Democratic challengers and open-seat candidates. Beyond this, Table 2.2 reaffirms what by now is a familiar diversity across PACs.[72]

It also reveals fluidity across time—a feature that was not as apparent in Table 2.1. To be sure, the overall pattern of support for Democratic incumbents is varied but fairly durable: In both years roughly a third allotted small proportions of their budgets (less than 20 percent) to these officeholders; about a third spent in the middle ranges (between 20 and 50 percent); a third or so were quite heavy supporters (50 percent or more of their contributions). Yet corporate PAC

Table 2.2
Spending Patterns of Corporate PACs in 1980 and 1984:
Budgetary Allotments to Four Types of Candidates

			Percent of Total Contributions					
From %	0–	10–	20–	30–	40–	50–	60–	Totals
To %	9	19	29	39	49	59	100	
			Democratic Incumbents					
1980 %	23.8	9.0	11.6	12.5	11.5	9.6	22.0	100.0%
(N)	(254)	(96)	(124)	(134)	(123)	(103)	(235)	1069
1984 %	20.7	7.4	10.2	10.2	11.4	11.2	28.9	100.0%
(N)	(304)	(108)	(149)	(150)	(168)	(164)	(425)	1468
			Republican Incumbents					
1980 %	21.0	11.9	17.7	19.9	14.0	6.6	8.9	100.0%
(N)	(224)	(127)	(189)	(213)	(150)	(71)	(95)	1069
1984 %	16.6	8.7	12.8	18.3	15.8	10.4	17.4	100.0%
(N)	(243)	(127)	(188)	(268)	(232)	(152)	(258)	1468
			Democratic Nonincumbents					
1980 %	89.9	5.4	2.3	.9	.4	.1	1.0	100.0%
(N)	(961)	(58)	(24)	(10)	(4)	(1)	(11)	1069
1984 %	95.5	2.6	.6	.3	.3	.1	.9	100.0%
(N)	(1397)	(38)	(9)	(4)	(4)	(1)	(15)	1468
			Republican Nonincumbents					
1980 %	32.4	15.1	13.4	10.1	9.6	5.5	13.9	100.0%
(N)	(346)	(161)	(143)	(108)	(103)	(59)	(149)	1069
1984 %	53.5	14.8	9.7	6.5	6.1	3.0	6.4	100.0%
(N)	(786)	(217)	(143)	(95)	(89)	(44)	(94)	1468

behavior toward Republicans is more nuanced, displaying both variation and instability. Clearly, sizable numbers of these organizations can be found in any given category of Republican support in any given year. One-fifth of all PACs in 1980 (and one-tenth in 1984) gambled at least half their budgets on Republican nonincumbents, even though the modal response—favored in 1980 by a third of all committees and in 1984 by over half—was to ignore these outsiders. This aggregate schizophrenia is mirrored in the distribution for GOP officeholders: Many committees gave large allotments in each year; many were not so generous. What is more, the temporal dimension adds a layer of complexity to these within-year patterns. The numbers show a clear shift away from Republican nonincumbents and toward Republican incumbents between elections.

A PAC Typology: Accommodationists, Partisans, and Adversaries

In their size and location, in their partisan coloration and in their preferences for incumbents or outsiders, it would appear that corporate PACs are an eclectic, even perplexing, assortment of political organizations. Of course, we eventually wish to argue that patterns like those of Table 2.2 are determined at least in part by the organizational differences between corporate PACs. But first we must find coherence in the patterns themselves. Drawing upon previous theoretical work,[73] we propose that three distinct contribution strategies—or, to stylize further, three types of PACs—are at work in our data.

Naturally, many corporate committees are indeed adept at playing the influence game, and they fit well the familiar fears of reformers. As it seeks through its contributions to reward a longtime congressional ally or perhaps to sway the vote of a prospective supporter, the *accommodationist* is easy to spot. Party is but a shopworn label and ideology is a fashionable cliché to this pragmatist. Its money is just as likely to find its way into the campaign coffers of powerful, senior incumbents on either side of the aisle. Of course it sometimes may pay to play the opportunist as well: An important incumbent in a close reelection bid might turn out to be especially grateful for a large donation. This subtlety aside, an ideal PAC world populated only with accommodationists would be revealed by its monotony: All committees would allot huge budgetary shares to Republican and Democratic incumbents.

We can see from the data that accommodation is probably an important element in accounting for the behavior of corporate PACs. Still, many organizations apparently do not accede so completely to the present realities of authority within Congress. They may in fact respond to motives of *opposition*—the desire to change what congressmen do by changing the composition of Congress. In its clearest and most recognizable form this desire takes shape in the straightforward strategies of *adversaries*. These opponents are like pragmatists turned on their heads. Suspicious, even disdainful of the congressional powers that be, and perhaps hoping to avenge a long litany of perceived governmental betrayals, the adversarial PAC searches for an elusive quality in would-be recipients— ideological purity. Moreover, in its ideal manifestation, an ideal quite frequently approached within the ranks of nonconnected PACs,[74] the adversary probably considers incumbency itself to be a corruption. Thus a corporate PAC world inhabited solely by adversaries would have its own singularity: It would be dominated by ardent advocates of right-wing nonincumbents, who have survived some "probusiness" ideological litmus test.

Strategies of opposition may take a more sophisticated form. For many corporate committees interested in changing the face of Congress, a candidate's incumbency status might be incidental and his ideology important but not decisive. What matters is his party. Compared to the adversary, the *partisan* PAC is more circumspect and realistic in its opposition. As a rule, a candidate's party affiliation, despite the occasional and celebrated exceptions, provides a fair approximation of his ideological leanings. And our ideal partisan finds a significance in the party label that transcends all but the most egregious departures from this rule. Party defines Congress in many important ways: leadership, committee assignments, informal organization, patterns of communications and discipline—all of these flow from party. And the corporate PAC partisan will see in the Republican party both the proper ideological legacy and the traditional means for institutional change. Its main goal, to work for and to protect Republican gains, requires that resources be deployed on two fronts. And so a PAC world comprised of Republican partisans would assume a two-dimensional quality: money would be spent both offensively, to support attractive Republican nonincumbents in winnable races, and defensively, to shore up endangered GOP incumbents facing formidable challenges.

We think that permitting the play of these three PAC types—accommodationists, adversaries, and partisans—adds plausibility to the observed contribution patterns and, as we have argued elsewhere, it may help us to understand changes in these patterns between elections.[75] Still, some difficulties arise in trying to distinguish the real-world behaviors of these three ideal PAC characters. After all, a single organization might pursue a *mix* of strategies, perhaps using some of its resources to spread goodwill among the powerful and some to back candidates it finds ideologically congenial. In fact the evidence suggests that corporate PACs may put their Democratic and Republican money to different purposes.[76] Thus we may wish at times to relax the useful simplification that the dominant strategy for any PAC fits one of the three main types.

Even with the aid of this simplifying assumption, however, the conceptually distinct styles of our three PAC personalities may be hard to detect empirically. For one thing, we have already seen that the climate of partisan expectations often conspires to produce conformity in the behavior of all types of contributors. For example if preelection auguries favor Democrats, both Republican partisans *and* accommodationists alike will move to support GOP incumbents—the former for reasons of partisan defense, the latter to seize an opportunity for future gratitude. If the tables turn and conditions favor Republicans, then the behaviors of Republican partisans and adversaries will be difficult to untangle, since both will be drawn to Republican nonincumbents. Furthermore, for a host of reasons, not the least of which is their aforementioned ability to extract support from contributors, substantial amounts of money from many PACs will end up with incumbents anyway. Hence, only the distinctive nonincumbent-oriented style of die-hard adversaries—subtlety is not their forte—will be clearly recognizable in the data.

Fortunately, incumbents are not all alike, and they differ in ways that make them more or less compatible with the preferences of accommodationists and partisans, and perhaps even adversaries. Some officeholders routinely win reelection or run unopposed, while others are chronically less secure. Some chair standing committees or are key ranking members, or even party leaders; most have lower visibility within the House. Some are known for their consistent and fairly extreme ideological positions; many maintain a more moderate or mixed set of views. Hence, even as PACs give to incumbents, they will frequently tip their hands. Accommodationists not only will be promiscuously bipartisan in their contributions, they will betray a special penchant for senior Democrats and Republicans in positions of authority. To the extent that they support incumbents at all, adversarial corporate PACs will aim for congressmen with proven and uncompromising conservative stands. And partisans will show a keener sensitivity than their adversarial and accommodationist comrades to the electoral histories (and possible fates) of Republican incumbents. Of course these expectations do not specify behaviors unique to each PAC type, but they do describe plausible if overlapping patterns. Is corporate PAC behavior toward incumbents differentiated in the ways our expectations would suggest?

Patterns of Incumbent Contributions: A Closer Look

Table 2.3 demonstrates the extent to which corporate PACs backed powerful House incumbents—the leadership of the Democratic and Republican parties, Democratic committee chairmen and ranking Republicans—in the 1983–1984 election cycle.[77] Table entries in the first column, for example, report the

Table 2.3
Corporate PAC Support of House Incumbents in 1984:
Percentage of PACs Targeting Specified Proportions of
Party Leaders and Committee Leaders

	Percentage distribution of PACs			
Proportion of a PAC's Democratic or Republican donees having attribute	Party leaders DEM (N=1249)	REP (N=1269)	Committee leaders DEM (N=1249)	REP (N=1269)
0	80.7%	74.9%	49.6%	45.7%
1-4	10.3	12.1	1.3	.7
5-9	4.1	6.6	10.3	6.3
10-14	1.8	3.0	16.5	13.6
15-19	.5	1.1	6.0	10.4
20-29	1.8	1.1	8.4	11.7
30-39	.4	.6	2.7	5.4
40-49	0	0	.6	.2
50-Over	.4	.7	4.6	6.1
Totals*	100.0%	100.1%	100.0%	100.1%

Note: 1.1 percent of all Democratic incumbents and 1.2 percent of all Republican incumbents are party leaders; 8.5 percent of all Democratic incumbents and 12.7 percent of all Republican incumbents are committee leaders.

*Column totals may not sum to 100.0% due to rounding error.

distribution that resulted from a simple computational question: Of the total number of Democratic incumbents that a PAC gave money to, what proportion held leadership positions in the Democratic party? If none of the Democratic incumbents a PAC supported was a party leader, that PAC would be categorized in the top row; if half or more were Democratic leaders, it would be placed in the bottom row, and so on. The same computations were then made for each committee's incumbent Republican recipients.

Thus the column percentages, when viewed in relation to the proportion of incumbents who have each attribute, sketch an interesting outline of what corporate PACs may have been aiming for. If a PAC targeted its incumbents at random in 1984, it would have "hit" a party leader scarcely more than 1 percent of the time (1.1 percent for Democrats and 1.2 percent for Republicans), a Democratic committee chair or ranking GOP member about 10 percent of the time (8.5 percent and 12.7 percent, respectively).

As we can see from Table 2.3, these base numbers provide an adequate portrayal of the preferences of many corporate PACs. The Democratic and Republican recipients of about 90 percent of all committees included none or very few leaders from either party's camp. The Democratic rosters of better than 60 percent of all PACs boasted unexceptional proportions (less than 10 percent) of committee chairs. And ranking members appeared less than 15 percent of the time on the Republican ledgers of two-thirds of all political action committees. But as is so often the case with corporate PACs, the modal tendencies tell only part of the story. The numbers for committee leaders taper off rather slowly toward the higher categories, especially on the GOP side; for almost one PAC in four the targeting of ranking Republicans occurred with suspicious frequency—at least 20 percent of the time. Democratic chairmen and the leaders of the two parties were not ignored, even assiduously courted, by some committees. Not surprisingly, the spirit of accommodation is alive and well in the contributions of quite a few PACs.

Furthermore, the fieldmarks of partisans—Republican partisans in particular—clearly appear in the data. In Table 2.4 we report the results of our computations for Democrats and Republicans in "marginal" reelection bids and for "junior" members of the House. To be sure, since a larger proportion of Republican incumbents (43 percent) than Democrats (only 26 percent) met our definition of marginal in 1984, the first two columns naturally center on different categories. Even allowing for this adjustment, however, the Republican column shows an uncanny symmetry, especially when compared to the heavily skewed Democratic distribution. In deciding which Republicans to support, precisely half of all corporate PACs revealed a preference for candidates with safe electoral histories; but the other half picked a marginal contest at least 50 percent of the time (and a remarkable 15.6 percent targeted a tough fight at least 90 percent of the time). Such instances of Democratic defense are rare events indeed.

These different partisan contours are echoed in patterns of support for candidates who enjoyed little seniority in 1984, those first elected to the House in

Table 2.4

Corporate PAC Support of House Incumbents in 1984:
Percentage of PACs Targeting Specified Proportions of
Marginal Members and Junior Members

| | Percentage distribution of PACs | | | |
| Proportion of a PAC's Democratic or Republican donees having attribute | Marginal members | | Junior members | |
	DEM (N=1249)	REP (N=1269)	DEM (N=1249)	REP (N=1269)
0-9	34.3%	16.4%	28.7%	18.0%
10-19	17.8	1.1	9.8	2.7
20-29	21.3	5.0	20.7	8.9
30-39	8.3	14.3	16.7	16.8
40-49	2.0	13.3	5.6	12.1
50-59	7.3	19.3	8.1	19.0
60-69	1.8	9.8	2.6	7.9
70-79	.6	4.0	.6	1.7
80-89	.1	1.2	.2	.6
90-Over	6.7	15.6	7.1	12.5
Totals*	100.2%	100.0%	100.1%	100.2%

Note: 25.9 percent of all Democratic incumbents and 43.0 percent of all Republican incumbents are marginal members; 31.1 percent of all Democratic incumbents and 38.8 percent of all Republican incumbents are junior members.

*Column totals may not sum to 100.0% due to rounding error.

1980 or 1982. Similar proportions of both groups of incumbents fit this criterion (31 percent of Democratic incumbents, 39 percent of the Republicans) and so the two distributions can be more directly compared. Again, although corporate committees gave ample support to Republicans with more seniority, the GOP rosters of over 40 percent of all PACs were at least half comprised of recently elected Republicans. (At least nine out of every ten candidates supported by a sizable minority—12.5 percent of all committees—were junior Republicans.) By comparison corporate PAC support for Democrats was one-dimensional. Indeed the general pattern of Table 2.4 suggests that, while accommodation assumes a Janus-like quality—the candidacies of sure winners and senior incumbents from both parties are well represented on the registers of corporate PACs—partisanship is more predictably a Republican phenomenon.

Table 2.5
Corporate PAC Support of House Incumbents in 1984:
Percentage Distribution of PACs by
Mean ACA and ADA Scores of Democratic and Republican Donees;
Percentage Distribution of ACA and ADA Scores of
All Democratic and Republican Incumbents

					ACA scores					
0-9	10-19	20-29	30-39	40-49	50-59	60-69	70-79	80-89	90-100	Totals* (N)
PACs, by mean score of Democratic donees										
4.3	16.1	24.3	23.6	14.6	11.1	4.5	1.0	.4	0	99.9% (1178)
Democratic incumbents										
20.8	26.1	16.4	13.0	3.9	5.8	5.8	4.8	1.9	1.4	99.9% (207)
PACs, by mean score of Republican donees										
.3	.3	0	1.2	1.2	5.0	9.6	39.0	27.4	16.0	100.0% (1214)
Republican incumbents										
.7	.7	0	5.7	4.3	7.8	5.7	24.8	21.3	29.1	100.1% (141)

					ADA scores					
0-9	10-19	20-29	30-39	40-49	50-59	60-69	70-79	80-89	90-100	Totals* (N)
PACs, by mean score of Democratic donees										
.6	4.3	6.6	11.1	13.8	16.6	16.8	15.5	10.2	4.4	99.9% (1178)
Democratic incumbents										
4.3	5.3	8.2	4.8	6.8	6.3	7.2	15.5	18.8	22.7	99.9% (207)
PACs, by mean score of Republican donees										
28.7	42.0	17.7	6.1	2.2	1.5	.7	.3	.9	0	100.1% (1214)
Republican incumbents										
35.5	30.5	11.3	7.1	3.5	5.7	3.5	.7	2.1	0	99.9% (141)

*Row percents may not sum to 100.0% due to rounding error.

Corporate PAC adversarialism, insofar as it manifests itself in incumbent contributions, is harder to find in our data. In Table 2.5 we present evidence on the ideological makeup of the officeholders supported by corporate PACs. These variables are based on the familiar ratings of the conservative Americans for Constitutional Action (ACA) and the liberal Americans for Democratic Action (ADA), but they are presented somewhat differently from the variables we have already discussed. The rows provide two sorts of information: the distribution of corporate PACs according to the *average* ACA and ADA scores of their Democratic and Republican recipients, and the "real-world" distribution of these scores for House Democrats and Republicans in 1984. Suppose for example that the mean ACA score for all incumbent Democrats supported by a PAC falls between 0 and 9.9. That committee would be entered in the left-most category of the top row. The second row provides a basis of comparison; it shows how all Democratic incumbents are distributed across the ACA rating. Thus while the ACA consigned one-fifth (20.8 percent) of all Democrats to the lowest category, the Democratic targets of barely 4 percent of all corporate PACs scored an average this low.

Is a profile of the adversarial corporate PAC etched within these figures? It is difficult to say for sure, but these patterns are not inconsistent with what we would expect from accommodationists (for whom questions of ideology rarely arise) and Republican partisans (whose targets on the whole should approximate party averages). The Republican rows of Table 2.5 show close conformity between PACs and GOP incumbents, and they bespeak remarkable unity among corporate committees. The Republican recipients of about 40 percent of all committees scored in the same range on the ACA and the ADA ratings; their scores came close to the overall averages; and there are no interesting departures from this pattern. For example, even though the ACA averages for fully 16 percent of corporate PACs registered in the conservative stratosphere (90 or better on the 100-point scale), there were plenty of targets (29.1 percent of all Republican incumbents) in that zone to begin with. If Republican adversaries are at work in these data, their preference for conservative candidates is camouflaged by the contribution styles of practically all corporate PACs.

The Democratic pattern, as usual, is different. To be sure, the data show that corporate committees were partial to Democrats more conservative than the norm. On the ACA variable, for example, nearly half of all House Democrats scored less than 20, yet the ones supported by nearly half of all PACs were more conservative, scoring between 20 and 40 on the 100-point scale. Similarly, on the ADA measure most Democratic incumbents are grouped in the higher scores, while most PACs gravitated toward the middle ranges. More telling than this conservative tilt, however, is the *spread* of the numbers. The Democratic rosters of corporate PACs had average scores that covered a broad range, especially on the ADA variable. This pattern is not incompatible with the suggestion that, for many PACs, a Democrat's ideology may be incidental to a choice that turns on other criteria.

Conclusion

Corporate PACs are denizens of an interesting world. To be sure, it is a place where the inhabitants share certain rudimentary characteristics. No corporate committee, after all, could be confused with a membership group, and all of them basically are staff driven. But it is the variety across corporate PACs that interests us. As we argued in the first part of this chapter, these organizations differ in ways that may determine what they do. Large PACs will be drawn in more than one direction. As with all organizations with superior resources they may lean toward greater staff autonomy and heightened innovation, but these tendencies will in many cases be tempered by the attendant trappings of size—a federated structure and (for a few) a Washington location. The hundreds of smaller committees will be more vulnerable to influential external forces, particularly the vagaries of the partisan climate or the blandishments of bellwethers. Finally, we think that ideology—a prominent feature in most accounts of group formation—is an important factor as well in explaining the creation and behavior of corporate PACs. Of course, like each of the dimensions we have stressed, the effect of ideas will be variable, not fixed. Yet unlike an acquired characteristic like budget size, the ideological impulse among corporate PACs, as we will show in the next chapter, is rather more like an inherited trait. Parents differ in whether they view their relations with government as harmful or benign, and they pass these views along to their PAC progeny.

Do political action committees behave in ways that reflect these organizational differences? That is the question to which we devote the remainder of the book. But as we saw in the second part of this chapter, corporate PACs in aggregate contour display the sort of variation one would expect from groups with differing internal arrangements. Some committees are large and spend freely; others are shoestring outfits with paltry budgets. Many give practically all of their money to incumbents; some allot the lion's share to challengers and open-seat candidates. Some are remarkably sensitive to interelection shifts in partisan fortunes; others change little over time.

This diversity, more importantly, suggests differentiation. Many corporate PACs are indeed obsequious pursuers of legislative purpose. Others, however, are more difficult to define in these terms. The behavior of many of these organizations bears the unmistakable earmarks of partisan motivation, particularly Republican partisanship. And a few—those that pursue "outside" strategies of supporting nonincumbents—betray an ideological bent. We now turn to the question of whether these outward signs are shaped by the internal lives of PACs and the dealings of their parent corporations with the federal government.

Notes

1. Frank J. Sorauf, "Who's in Charge? Accountability in Political Action Committees," *Political Science Quarterly* 99 (Winter 1984–1985), pp. 591–614; Larry J. Sabato, *PAC Power* (New York: W. W. Norton and Co., 1985); John R. Wright, "PACs, Contributions, and Roll Calls: An Organizational Perspective," *American Political Science Review* 79, no. 2 (June 1985), pp. 400–14.

2. David B. Truman, *The Governmental Process*, 2d ed. (New York: Alfred A. Knopf, 1971), first published in 1951; Mancur Olson, Jr., *The Logic of Collective Action* (Cambridge: Harvard University Press, 1965); James Q. Wilson, *Political Organizations* (New York: Basic Books, 1973); Robert H. Salisbury, "An Exchange Theory of Interest Groups," *Midwest Journal of Political Science* 13, no. 1 (February 1969), pp. 1–32; Albert O. Hirschman, *Exit, Voice, and Loyalty* (Cambridge: Harvard University Press, 1970); Terry M. Moe, *The Organization of Interests* (Chicago: University of Chicago Press, 1980);

Jeffrey M. Berry, *Lobbying for the People* (Princeton, NJ: Princeton University Press, 1977); Jack L. Walker, "The Origins and Maintenance of Interest Groups in America," *American Political Science Review* 77, no. 2 (June 1983), pp. 390–406.

3. Thomas L. Gais, Mark A. Peterson, and Jack L. Walker, "Interest Groups, Iron Triangles, and Representative Institutions in American National Government," *British Journal of Political Science* 14, no. 2 (April 1984), pp. 166–67.

4. Walker, "The Origins and Maintenance of Interest Groups in America," pp. 391–92.

5. Kay L. Schlozman and John T. Tierney, *Organized Interests and American Democracy* (New York: Harper and Row, 1986), p. 82.

6. Robert H. Salisbury, "Interest Representation: The Dominance of Institutions," *American Political Science Review* 78, no. 1 (March 1984), p. 64.

7. Salisbury, "Interest Representation," pp. 67–68.

8. Salisbury, "Interest Representation," p. 70.

9. Salisbury, "Interest Representation," p. 75.

10. Charles Perrow, "Members as Resources in Voluntary Associations," in Walter R. Rosengren, ed., *Organizations and Clients* (Columbus, OH: Charles E. Merrill, 1970), pp. 93–116.

11. Wilson, *Political Organizations*, pp. 217–18.

12. Berry, *Lobbying for the People*; Andrew S. McFarland, *Public Interest Lobbies* (Washington, DC: American Enterprise Institute for Public Policy Research, 1976).

13. Walker, "The Origins and Maintenance of Interest Groups in America," p. 404.

14. Michael T. Hayes, "The New Group Universe," in Allan J. Cigler and Burdett A. Loomis, eds., *Interest Group Politics*, 2d ed. (Washington, DC: Congressional Quarterly Press, 1986), pp. 133–45. Hayes's typology suggests that the interaction of two organizational variables, primary source of financial support (member sources/outside sources) and opportunity for face-to-face relations (high/low), defines four sorts of groups: pure membership groups (membership/high), mass groups (membership/low), subsidized solidary groups (outside/high), and pure staff groups (outside/low). See also Hayes, *Lobbyists and Legislators* (New Brunswick, NJ: Rutgers University Press, 1981), pp. 71–92.

15. Theodore J. Eismeier and Philip H. Pollock III, "An Organizational Analysis of Political Action Committees," *Political Behavior* 7, no. 2 (1985), pp. 192–216.

16. Sorauf, "Who's in Charge? Accountability in Political Action Committees," pp. 605–6.

17. Berry, *Lobbying for the People*, pp. 187–88.

18. Edward Handler and John R. Mulkern, *Business in Politics: Campaign Strategies of Corporate Political Action Committees* (Lexington, MA: Lexington Books, 1982), p. 70.

19. Sorauf, "Who's in Charge? Accountability in Political Action Committees," pp. 594–95.

20. Sabato, *PAC Power*, p. 35.

21. Handler and Mulkern, *Business in Politics*, p. 71.

22. Schlozman and Tierney, *Organized Interests and American Democracy*, pp. 226–31; Sabato, *PAC Power*, pp. 41–42.

23. Berry, *Lobbying for the People*, pp. 208–9; Wilson, *Political Organizations*, pp. 224–32; McFarland, *Public Interest Lobbies*, p. 55.

24. Sabato, *PAC Power*, pp. 29–31.

25. Edwin M. Epstein, "The PAC Phenomenon: An Overview-Introduction." *Arizona Law Review* 22, no. 2 (1980), p. 367.

26. Wilson, *Political Organizations*, pp. 210–11.

27. Handler and Mulkern, *Business in Politics*, pp. 24–26. Eismeier and Pollock, "Political Action Committees: Varieties of Organization and Strategy," in Michael J. Malbin, ed., *Money and Politics in the United States* (Chatham, NJ: Chatham House, 1984), pp. 122–141.

28. Wilson, *Political Organizations*, p. 210.

29. Eismeier and Pollock, "Political Action Committees: Varieties of Organization and Strategy," pp. 125–26.

30. Hayes, *Lobbyists and Legislators*, p. 80.

31. Truman, *The Governmental Process*, p. 115.

32. Truman, *The Governmental Process*, p. 118.

33. Truman, *The Governmental Process*, pp. 122–23.

34. This expectation parallels Malbin's argument about the effects of economic diversification on PAC allocations. Michael J. Malbin, "Campaign Financing and the 'Special Interests,'" *The Public Interest* 56 (December 1979), pp. 21–42.

35. Wright, "PACs, Contributions, and Roll Calls," pp. 403–4.

36. Wright, "PACs, Contributions, and Roll Calls," p. 400.

37. Truman, *The Governmental Process*, p. 117.

38. Seymour Martin Lipset, Martin Trow, and James Coleman, *Union Democracy* (Garden City, NY: Anchor Books, 1956).

39. Olson, *The Logic of Collective Action*.

40. Salisbury, "An Exchange Theory of Interest Groups"; Wilson, *Political Organizations*; Moe, *The Organization of Interests*.

41. Wilson, *Political Organizations*, p. 197.

42. Walker, "The Origins and Maintenance of Interest Groups in America," p. 398.

43. Sabato, *PAC Power*, pp. 29–31.

44. Quoted by Sabato, *PAC Power*, p. 30.

45. Handler and Mulkern, *Business in Politics*, p. 101.

46. See Howard Margolis, *Selfishness, Altruism, and Rationality* (Chicago: University of Chicago Press, 1982), p. 100.

47. Handler and Mulkern, *Business in Politics*, p. 102.

48. Moe, *The Organization of Interests*, pp. 191–99.

49. Handler and Mulkern, *Business in Politics*, p. 105.

50. Wilson, *Political Organizations*, p. 10.

51. Wilson, *Political Organizations*, p. 263.

52. Eismeier and Pollock, "An Organizational Analysis of Political Action Committees," pp. 207–9.

53. Eismeier and Pollock, "An Organizational Analysis of Political Action Committees," p. 199.

54. Handler and Mulkern, *Business in Politics*, pp. 94–96.

55. Sabato, *PAC Power*, pp. 55–56.

56. Sorauf, "Who's in Charge? Accountability in Political Action Committees," p. 608.

57. Wilson, *Political Organizations*, p. 262.

58. Sabato, *PAC Power*, pp. 46–47.

59. Handler and Mulkern, *Business in Politics*, pp. 99–100.

60. Sabato, *PAC Power*, p. 46.

61. Frank J. Sorauf, "Varieties of Experience: Campaign Finance in the House and

Senate," in Kay Lehman Schlozman, ed., *Elections in America* (Boston: Allen and Unwin, 1987), pp. 197–218. See esp. pp. 204–8.

62. David Adamany, "Political Parties in the 1980's," in Malbin, ed., *Money and Politics in the United States*, pp. 70–121.

63. See Thomas B. Edsall, "If You've Got the Dime, Coelho's Got the Ear," *Washington Post National Weekly Edition*, December 23, 1985.

64. Gary C. Jacobson and Samuel J. Kernell, *Strategy and Choice in Congressional Elections* (New Haven, CT: Yale University Press, 1981).

65. For a particularly enthusiastic overstatement of the tendency for political action committees to contribute to incumbents—and for a condemnation of the role of money in general—see Amitai Etzioni, *Capital Corruption* (New York: Harcourt Brace Jovanovich, 1984).

66. Edie N. Goldenberg and Michael W. Traugott, *Campaigning for Congress* (Washington, D.C.: Congressional Quarterly Press, 1984), p. 94.

67. Eismeier and Pollock, "A Tale of Two Elections: PAC Money in 1980 and 1984," *Corruption and Reform* 1 (1986), pp. 189–207.

68. Fred Wertheimer, "The PAC Phenomenon in American Politics," *Arizona Law Review* 22, no. 2 (1980), p. 605.

69. Epstein, "The PAC Phenomenon: An Overview-Introduction."

70. The general campaign finance data used in this chapter, and throughout the entire book, were obtained from the Federal Election Commission's 1979–1980 and 1983–1984 candidate and nonparty committee (that is, PAC) data tapes. The FEC files, which are remarkably detailed, summarize the reported transactions between every candidate and every political action committee in the election cycle. In addition to information specific to the transaction (e.g., the amount of the contribution), the FEC records include data for the PAC (total contributions to all candidates, FEC classification, state, etc.) and candidate (House or Senate, party, incumbency status, district, etc.). We sorted these files by each PAC's identification number and obtained aggregated information for each committee. To investigate certain questions we found it useful to augment the FEC data with information obtained from other sources. We take note of these where appropriate. Also, unless otherwise noted, all data reported in this book are for general election House candidacies only, and all dollar amounts reflect direct PAC-to-candidate contributions.

71. In 1980, forty-nine corporate committees (4.6 percent of the total) could be given this "inside the Beltway" designation; in 1984, ninety-one PACs (6.2 percent).

72. For an argument that this diversity masks a high degree of business unity see Dan Clawson, Alan Neustadl, and James Bearden, "The Logic of Business Unity: Corporate Contributions in the 1980 Congressional Elections," *American Sociological Review* 51, no. 6 (December 1986), pp. 797–811. However, the evidence adduced here shows not that corporate PACs are alike in important strategic behavior but that they share an entirely reasonable aversion to helpless challengers.

73. Jacobson and Kernell, *Strategy and Choice in Congressional Elections*.

74. For an excellent discussion of nonconnected PACs, see Margaret Ann Latus, "Assessing Ideological PACs: From Outrage to Understanding," in Malbin, ed., *Money and Politics in the United States*, pp. 142–171.

75. Eismeier and Pollock, "Strategy and Choice in Congressional Elections: The Role of Political Action Committees," *American Journal of Political Science* 30, no. 1 (February 1986), pp. 197–213.

76. Eismeier and Pollock, "A Tale of Two Elections: PAC Money in 1980 and 1984."

77. For Tables 2.3, 2.4, and 2.5 we augmented our basic data set with information on incumbent characteristics, compiled from Michael Barone and Grant Ujifusa, *The Almanac of American Politics 1984* (Washington, DC: National Journal, 1983). For Table 2.3, the speaker, majority leader, minority leader, and the Democratic and Republican whips are all considered party leaders; committee leadership is determined by chairmanship or ranking member status on any standing committee. For Table 2.4, incumbents first elected in 1980 or 1982 are considered "junior" in our data; and any incumbent elected or reelected in 1982 by less than 60 percent of the vote is "marginal." For Table 2.5, we used the Americans for Constitutional Action (ACA) and Americans for Democratic Action (ADA) ratings, both from 1982, to tap the conservative or liberal inclinations of incumbents.

3

PACs and the Politics of Regulation

The beginning of wisdom about corporate PACs is that they are not all of a piece. In their size, structure, strategy, and tactics these organizations are strikingly diverse, more diverse certainly than their counterparts parented by trade associations and labor unions. Yet there is also a pattern in this mosaic, which is revealed by an appreciation of the manifold ways in which government has come to affect American business.

Government, after all, has been the twentieth century's most remarkable growth industry. The most obvious measure of this growth is fiscal, for in its taxing, spending, and borrowing the public economy now has profound effects on private economic activity. Moreover, a host of products have come to be protected and promoted in international markets, and domestic markets have been shaped by an expanding regulatory maze.

Thus, despite its often expressed disdain for politics, American business has become increasingly enmeshed in political activities. The creation of some 1,500 corporate PACs in the last decade is one manifestation of this involvement, but there are other widely remarked measures as well. In many corporations the public affairs function has gained new prominence. The number of firms with Washington outposts now stands at more than 600, and thousands more have some form of representation in Washington.[1] Moreover, political activity has not been limited to Washington; several hundred companies have embarked on ambitious projects of constituency building and grass-roots political organizing among employees.[2]

The political activism of corporations in the 1970s and 1980s has been described as "one of the most remarkable campaigns in the pursuit of political power in recent history."[3] Yet to call all of this a campaign may be to impute too much organization and singleness of purpose to it. Clearly much of this activity has been politics as usual—the pursuit of access and the cementing of established political relationships to secure firm-specific or industry-specific benefits—only updated to a changed legal and political environment. And in many cases the new political resources of corporations have been used in competition with one another:

> Thus, General Electric and United Technologies are in competition for military jet engine contracts. Boeing, Lockheed, and McDonnell Douglas have waged well publicized campaigns to build a new military cargo plane. Auto dealers have tried to get Congress to block Detroit's discounts to fleet buyers. Big business and small business are at odds over the Administration's proposal to weaken affirmative action requirements. The sugar industry has supported bans on aspartame and saccharin. The maritime industry and farm interests disagree about whether food aid must travel in U.S.-flag vessels. Money market funds are opposed to banks' attempts to enter the mutual fund business. Northwest Airlines is fighting the transfer of Pan Am's Pacific routes to United Airlines.[4]

However, the growing political activity of business has not been limited to the politics of pragmatism. In word and deed much of this activity has taken a decidedly confrontational stance in opposition to the recent course of public policy. Such opposition is evident in some of the estimated $1 billion of issue advertising purchased annually by business and in the $6 million in venture capital spent by corporate PACs on Republican challengers in the congressional races of 1980.

There is, we have seen, evidence of accommodation, partisanship, and adversarialism in the contributions of corporate PACs. In most recent elections incumbent Democrats in the House have received as much or more from corporate PACs as incumbent Republicans. Democratic challengers, however, have received virtually no money from corporate PACs. Republican challengers, especially those in Senate races, have on occasion received large infusions of money from these PACs. These aggregate spending patterns reflect the great diversity in the spending patterns of individual PACs, which range from staunch Republicanism to a consistent and bipartisan favoring of incumbents. These strategic and tactical differences among PACs are in part the product of the diverse experiences of their parent corporations with government policies, especially with regulatory policies.

The Politics of Regulation

Government regulation of the American economy has come in three great waves: at the turn of the century with legislation regulating trusts and working conditions as well as the establishment of the Interstate Commerce Commission and Federal Trade Commission; during the New Deal with regulation of the securities and banking industries as well as labor–management relations; and in the 1960s and 1970s with the creation of new regulatory institutions such as the Environmental Protection Agency, the Consumer Product Safety Commission, and the Occupational Safety and Health Administration.

It has been widely remarked that the last of these periods of government activity represented a fundamental change in regulatory philosophy.[5] Economic regulations adopted during the first two eras tended to be industry-specific— securities, banking, trucking, railroads, utilities, communications, and others— and they had as their primary concerns the structure of markets, price rates, and the obligation to serve. The so-called social regulations of the 1970s, on the other hand, were intended to affect the conditions under which goods and services are produced and the condition of products that are manufactured. The newly established agencies cast a wide regulatory net—health and working conditions, environmental quality, and highway safety were among their chief concerns—and they set standards that, unlike economic regulation, cut across industry bounds.

Following the distinction between old and new styles of regulation, there has been careful economic analysis of the problems and possibilities of achieving the complex objectives of social regulation.[6] Analysis of the political implications of the evolution in regulatory policy has made a sharp distinction between the harmony of business–government relations under old-style economic regulation and the hostility of those relations under new-style social regulation. Drawn too sharply such a distinction loses important nuances in the histories of particular regulatory policies and agencies,[7] but it does serve as a useful shorthand to identify several specific differences between older and newer regulations.

To begin with, the regulatory policies of the 1970s tended to be born of a different politics than those of earlier periods. The most useful typology of regulatory politics is James Q. Wilson's, which distinguishes among policies according to the perceived incidence of their costs and benefits.[8] Traditional economic regulation was often the product of *client politics* with the benefits of policy concentrated and the costs widely distributed. It is this brand of politics, of course, that most closely conforms to the "capture" theory of regulation— organized producer groups turning regulations to their advantage at the expense of unorganized consumers. Firms within affected industries may view economic regulation as a way to help stabilize and rationalize relationships with their competitors and with government, and such industries have good reason to cultivate their relationships with the congressional overseers of the regulatory apparatus.

Many of the recent pieces of social regulation, in contrast, were the products of *entrepreneurial politics*. Entrepreneurial politics are generated by proposed policies with perceived benefits that are widely distributed and perceived costs that are concentrated in particular segments of industry. Thus by one estimate 70 percent of the $6.6 billion pollution-related investment for 1975 was made by the utilities, petroleum refining, chemicals, nonferrous metals, and paper industries; a similarly high percentage of the $4 billion expense for enhancing worker safety fell on the chemicals, metals, wood, paper, and automobile industries.[9] The regulations proposed in the second half of this decade have similarly concentrated costs.[10]

Since opponents of such policies would seem to have more incentive to organize than beneficiaries, it is surprising that such regulatory legislation of this sort was enacted in such volume during the 1970s. That it was, Wilson argues, was the result of the development of a new class of

> skilled entrepreneur who can mobilize latent public sentiment (by revealing a scandal or capitalizing on a crisis), put the opponents of the plan publicly on the defensive (by accusing them of deforming babies or killing motorists), and associate the proposed legislation with widely shared values (clean air, pure water, health, and safety). The entrepreneur serves as the vicarious representative of groups not directly part of the legislative process. Ralph Nader was such an entrepreneur and the Auto Safety Act of 1966 was one result.[11]

By its very nature entrepreneurial politics tends, at least at the formative stages of regulation, to be adversarial, replete with proclaimed victims and villains.

Related to the circumstances of their creation is a difference in the implementation of the new social regulations. The economic regulations of the turn of the century and the 1930s, Table 3.1 shows, were for the most part created by brief general statutes and administered with broad discretion by independent commissions. In part as a reaction to the perceived inadequacies of this system, the drafters of regulations in the 1970s wrote explicit and detailed legislation and deliberately placed authority for implementation in the hands of agencies of the executive branch, which presumably would be more accountable to Congress.[12] These agencies in turn have had to find ways of coping with the ambitious mandates of legislation and, according to Paul W. MacAvoy, have done so:

> Although goals were set in terms of improving health and safety across the country, EPA, NHTSA, and OSHA regulations evolved away from performance to setting out and partially enforcing detailed equipment specifications. Because standard setting has been litigious and prolonged, the existing set of rules has not been complete. But these regulations when available and applied to the individual plant have proven to be extremely detailed and inflexible.[13]

Many of these specifications—OSHA provided the most notorious examples— became symbols of bureaucratic imperialism.

All of this was regarded by many in the business community as much more than a mere annoyance. Unlike earlier economic regulations, the new social

Table 3.1
Major Regulatory Agencies in the United States:
Year Established and Administrative Location

Agency	Year	Location
Interstate Commerce Commission	1887	Independent
Antitrust Division of Justice Department	1890	Executive Branch
Federal Trade Commission	1914	Independent
International Trade Commission	1916	Independent
Federal Power Commission	1920	Independent
Food and Drug Administration	1931	Independent
Federal Home Loan Bank Board	1932	Independent
Federal Deposit Insurance Corporation	1933	Independent
Federal Communications Commission	1934	Independent
Securities and Exchange Commission	1934	Independent
National Labor Relations Board	1934	Independent
Federal Maritime Commission	1936	Independent
Civil Aeronautics Board	1938	Independent
Federal Aviation Administration	1948	Executive Branch
Equal Employment Opportunity Commission	1964	Independent
National Transportation Safety Board	1966	Executive Branch
Federal Railroad Administration	1966	Executive Branch
Environmental Protection Agency	1970	Executive Branch
National Highway Traffic Safety Admin.	1970	Executive Branch
Occupational Safety and Health Admin.	1970	Executive Branch
Consumer Product Safety Commission	1972	Independent
Nuclear Regulatory Commission	1973	Independent
Mine Safety and Health Administration	1973	Executive Branch
Office of Surface Mining Reclamation and Enforcement	1977	Executive Branch
Economic Regulatory Administration	1977	Executive Branch

Sources: Alfred Marcus, The Adversary Economy (Westport, Connecticut: Quorum Books, 1984), pp. 40-41; Lawrence J. White, Reforming Regulation: Processes and Problems (Englewood Cliffs, New Jersey: Prentice Hall, 1981), pp. 32-33, pp. 36-39.

regulation had a pervasiveness and intrusiveness that came to be regarded in some quarters as serious threats to business prerogatives and perhaps more importantly to the balance of power between business and nonbusiness interests.[14] Such concerns were abetted by general economic conditions and legitimized by political rhetoric that linked the problem of a malfunctioning economy to the problem of malfunctioning big government.[15]

The political consequences of the old-style economic regulations are plain enough; firms in regulated industries can be expected to accommodate themselves to the realities of power in Washington. The political implications of the new social regulation, however, are less obvious. It has been argued that adversarialism of the type commonly practiced by regulatory entrepreneurs begets an adversarial response by the regulated.[16] Others, however, have suggested that rather than simply railing against social regulations, firms within affected industries ought to seek competitive advantage in their response to government policies.[17] And even where regulations are onerous, the most effective response might well be political entrepreneurship by corporations in dealing with the regulatory bureaucracy and its congressional watchdogs.[18] Indeed, much of the new political activism of corporations represents not a dramatic departure from the traditional politics of pragmatism but a more self-conscious application of these skills.[19]

This suggests that the rhetoric, campaign activity, and lobbying of corporations are likely to contain different mixtures of accommodation and adversarialism. To be sure, the PACs of most firms, including the self-proclaimed victims of social regulation, may be in part linked to lobbying activities and used to reward allies in Congress. For several reasons, however, the PACs of the newly regulated might also be used as instruments of political resistance. Corporate PACs, we saw in Chapter 2, may be harnessed to public affairs activities, but they may also be expressive of the ideologies of individual contributors. In fact, in many corporations the PAC is a very small operation, and in many it is entirely in the hands of nonspecialist amateurs.[20] Moreover, there is some evidence that Congress is a less useful arena of power for the newly regulated than for the traditionally regulated. In one recent sample, the percentage of firms reporting significant influence before regulatory bodies hovered around 50 percent for all industries. However, much greater variation across industries was reported in regard to influence in Congress. Almost two-thirds of utilities and half of firms in financial services reported significant influence before Congress; a third or less of firms in high technology, energy, and mining reported such influence.[21] Without much to lose such firms might be inclined to take the position described by a public affairs official of an oil company:

> In the 1980 contest we gave heavily to challengers. And drastically reduced the amount of our giving to incumbents. In fact, we often went right up to the limit with challengers. We have found that politicians have more respect for your point of view if the company takes a stand. Otherwise, Washington doesn't think much of the firm.[22]

Thus the political economy of corporate PACs is at once richly textured yet partially explicable in terms of differing regulatory experiences. As a first approximation, we expect the PACs whose parents reside in industries of traditional regulation—transportation, communications, and financial services—to be more accommodationist than PACs from sectors that are not subjects of such controls. As a second approximation we expect the PACs whose parents have been primary targets of social regulation—mining and construction and much of the manufacturing sector, especially chemicals, lumber and paper, and machinery—to be more inclined to pursue tactics of opposition. PACs from industries that are subject to both types of regulation—utilities, for example—will, one might expect, choose pragmatism over indignation and pursue an accommodationist strategy.[23]

Industries and firms may be differentially affected by other policies as well, including special provisions of the tax code and protection from foreign competition.[24] The relationship of firms to politics may also be affected by the fact that they are major government contractors or that their PACs are located in the insider's world along the Potomac. Do such cross-pressures produce distinctive patterns in the ways in which PACs spend their money? A definitive answer requires systematic analysis of the universe of PACs, a task to which we now turn.

Patterns of Corporate PAC Spending in 1980 and 1984

In Chapter 2 we distinguished three ideal types of corporate PACs—accommodationists, partisans, and adversaries—and suggested that the diversity in the spending patterns of these PACs reveals different mixes of strategies. Here we have argued that PAC strategies are likely to vary from industry to industry, with PACs from industries that enjoy beneficial relations with government leaning toward accommodation and PACs from industries that chafe under government regulation more likely to pursue strategies of partisanship or adversarialism. Of course, regulatory experiences and other industry-specific differences do not explain all of the variation in PAC strategies. There is, we have found, much that is idiosyncratic, even vagarious in how PACs spend their money.

If industry differences are robust enough, however, they ought to survive elementary statistical controls and stand out above what we know to be a great deal of noise in the system of corporate PACs. To determine whether there are such differences we have examined in some detail the spending patterns of corporate PACs in the House elections of 1980 and 1984. The dominance of the Democratic party and the great advantages of incumbents, 90 percent or more of whom typically win reelection, make accommodation the norm in House elections. Still, in 1980, and to a lesser extent in 1984, favorable conditions, including strength at the top of the ticket, produced some risk taking among corporate PACs. In 1980, 29 percent of the spending of corporate PACs in House elections went to Republican challengers and open-seat races. In 1984, 17 percent of the budget of corporate PACs went to these candidates. The data sets, which include for each election all corporate PACs that spent more than $2,500 on House races, allow us to see which sorts of PACs were inclined to take such risks and which leaned toward Republican or Democratic incumbents.[25]

Each PAC was classified according to the nature of business of its parent corporation, as defined by the Department of Commerce's Standard Industrial

Code.[26] Some PACs, it should be noted, represent corporations with more than one Standard Industrial Code, in which case the regression models reported here estimate the net effect of being in several different industry types as the sum of the specific industry effects. Dummy variables are included to test for the effect of being a major defense contractor as well as that of having the PAC headquartered in Washington, D.C. We also wish to allow for the possibility that, contrary to popular stereotypes, many smaller PACs may have stronger local than national ties. Thus we include as control the percentage of the delegation of the state in which the PAC is headquartered that is Democratic.[27]

Table 3.2 counts the number of firms doing business in various industries that had PACs that spent at least $2,500 in House races in 1980 and 1984, with multiple counts for those firms whose business spanned more than one industrial classification. Several industries within the manufacturing sector are among

Table 3.2
Number of PACs Representing Firms from Various Industries,
1980 and 1984 House Elections

Industry:	Number of PACs* 1980	1984
Mining		
minerals	35	33
coal	28	28
oil & gas extraction	95	100
Construction	49	53
Manufacturing		
tobacco manufactures	4	4
textile mill products	38	34
apparel	12	12
lumber & paper	68	69
chemicals	130	139
petroleum & coal	40	42
rubber & plastics	80	80
primary metals	89	90
fabricated metals	117	125
machinery	141	147
electrical equipment	107	115
transportation equipment	88	97
Transportation		
railroads	23	22
local & interurban	7	8
trucking & warehousing	24	29
water transportation	18	24
air transportation	30	27
Utilities	101	131
Communications	52	59
Finance		
banking	131	167
credit agencies	51	65
securities & commodities	17	26
insurance carriers	52	61

*Includes for each election PACs that spent more than $2500 in House races. There are multiple counts for PACs with corporate parents that do business in more than one industry.

those with the largest number of PACs, as is oil and gas extraction. PACs from industries subject to traditional economic controls—utilities, communication, and finance—are also numerous and have grown the fastest since 1980. Well represented are defense contractors, the largest of which contributed over $4 million to House elections in 1984. The gross numbers of PACs in different industries reflect previously identified sectoral variation in rates of participation in PACs.[28]

Reported in Table 3.3 are the estimated effects on the spending allocations of a PAC having a corporate parent doing business in various industries, with controls for the partisan composition of the delegation of the state in which the PAC is located as well as for whether the PAC is headquartered in Washington

Table 3.3
Sectoral Variation in Budget Allocations, 1980 House Elections:
Unstandardized Regression Coefficients and t-Ratios for PACs in Different Industries

	Dependent variables: Percent of budget to		
Industry:	Democratic incumbents	Republican incumbents	Republican non-incumb.
Mining			
minerals	5.3 (1.1)	−1.0 (−0.3)	−4.0 (−0.8)
coal	5.4 (1.1)	−3.1 (−0.9)	−6.4 (−1.3)
oil & gas	−9.5 (−3.1)	−1.4 (−0.7)	9.8 (3.2)
Construction	−5.6 (−1.4)	0.5 (0.2)	4.0 (1.0)
Manufacturing			
tobacco	31.6 (2.4)	−9.7 (−1.1)	−22.6 (−1.7)
textiles	−3.1 (−0.7)	−1.1 (−0.4)	4.4 (0.9)
apparel	6.9 (0.9)	7.7 (1.4)	−13.2 (−1.7)
lumber & paper	−5.9 (1.7)	1.1 (0.4)	5.6 (1.7)
chemicals	−2.9 (−1.1)	1.4 (0.8)	2.2 (0.9)
petroleum & coal	−3.0 (−0.7)	2.6 (0.9)	1.0 (0.2)
rubber & plastics	−8.3 (−2.5)	5.3 (2.4)	3.4 (1.0)
primary metals	1.8 (0.5)	1.3 (0.6)	−3.0 (−0.9)
fabricated metals	−4.0 (−1.2)	4.1 (1.8)	0.4 (0.1)
machinery	−6.2 (−2.1)	−1.5 (−0.7)	7.6 (2.6)
electrical equip.	1.0 (0.3)	0.2 (0.1)	−0.8 (−0.3)
transportation equip.	0.1 (0.1)	−1.1 (−0.5)	0.8 (0.4)
Transportation			
railroads	8.9 (1.6)	−0.3 (−0.1)	−8.3 (−1.5)
local & interurban	−23.4 (−1.8)	9.2 (1.0)	16.7 (1.3)
trucking & warehousing	5.7 (1.1)	0.1 (0.1)	−5.8 (−1.1)
water transportation	15.6 (2.6)	0.9 (0.2)	−15.2 (−2.6)
air transportation	19.0 (3.7)	−1.1 (−0.3)	−17.3 (−3.4)
Utilities	8.7 (3.0)	−3.7 (−1.9)	−4.6 (−1.6)
Communications	4.5 (1.2)	4.5 (1.8)	−10.2 (−2.8)
Finance			
banking	9.6 (2.5)	−8.4 (−3.2)	−8.1 (−2.1)
credit agencies	11.5 (2.4)	−1.0 (−0.3)	−12.9 (−2.7)
securities	8.9 (1.3)	0.2 (0.1)	−7.3 (−1.1)
insurance carriers	0.1 (0.1)	−2.2 (−0.7)	1.1 (0.3)
Washington office	9.4 (2.0)	−1.5 (−0.5)	−6.7 (−1.4)
Defense contractor	11.0 (2.8)	3.3 (1.2)	−14.7 (−3.8)
Percent Democratic,			
homestate delegation	24.6 (4.9)	−27.0 (−7.8)	0.8 (0.2)
Constant	22.2	46.7	29.4
	R^2=.20	R^2=.16	R^2=.15
	N=685	N=685	N=685

and whether or not the parent corporation is among the top fifty contractors of the Department of Defense.[29] As expected, these factors were important influences on spending decisions. PACs in states with high proportions of Democrats in the House delegation tended on average to give substantially more to Democratic incumbents and substantially less to Republican incumbents than PACs in states with lower proportions of Democrats. This reflects the apparently strong local pulls on PACs, about which we will have more to say in Chapter 4. Compared to other corporate PACs, those headquartered along the Potomac allocated on average almost 10 percent more to Democratic incumbents and 7 percent less to Republican challengers and candidates for open seats. Those PACs representing the largest defense contractors were inclined to incumbents of both parties, but especially Democrats. On average they gave 15 percent less of their budgets to Republican nonincumbents than other corporate PACs.

Along with these influences Table 3.3 shows differences across industries that, with some interesting anomalies, conform to expectations. The spending allocations of PACs from sectors of traditional economic regulation—transportation, utilities, communications, and finance—betray very strong accommodationist sentiments. By and large the PACs representing these nonindustrials spent substantially less on Republican nonincumbents and substantially more on incumbent Democrats. Excluding local and interurban transit, for which there are very few cases, PACs from the transportation sector gave, on average, 6 to 19 percent more of their budgets to Democratic incumbents than other PACs and from 6 to 17 percent less to Republican challengers and open seats. The PACs of the banking, credit, and securities industries all gave about 10 percent more on average to Democratic incumbents, as did the PACs of utilities. The communications industry also tilted toward incumbents, albeit in a more bipartisan fashion. Clearly, sector-specific regulation seems to incline PACs toward political accommodation generally, and toward accommodation of Democrats in particular.

The distinctive style of Democratic accommodation that is the hallmark of the beneficiaries of old-style regulation is virtually absent from spending patterns of almost all other groups of PACs in the analysis. PACs representing the construction industry and most of the industries in the manufacturing sector show a much stronger preference for Republicans and, in some instances, a penchant for GOP challengers and open-seat candidates. Moreover, those manufacturing industries that depart most sharply from this pattern—tobacco products in its decided tilt toward Democratic incumbents and the apparel industry in its heavy giving to incumbents of both parties—are obvious claimants of subsidies or protection and thus exceptions that help prove the rule.

Of the manufacturing PACs, chemicals, lumber and paper, rubber, fabricated metals, and machinery—all self-proclaimed victims of new-style social regulation—channeled relatively small amounts of their money into the campaigns of Democratic incumbents in 1980. Virtually all of these PACs, of course, preferred Republicans, and some displayed notable bias toward GOP nonincumbents. Thus on average a PAC from the machinery sector located in a state with a typical partisan division of the congressional delegation spent almost 40 percent of its budget for House races on Republican nonincumbents, significantly more than the share of the aggregate spending of corporate PACs that went to these candidates. Textile PACs, with the cross pressures of regulation and possible protection, joined in these oppositional tactics. Transportation equipment PACs, with similar constraints, did not and neither did the PACs from the electronic equipment sector, some of which have entered the political market only recently.[30]

Outside manufacturing are interesting cases as well. As expected, construction PACs shunned accommodation, contributing relatively small shares of their

Table 3.4
Sectoral Variation in Budget Allocations, 1984 House Elections:
Unstandardized Regression Coefficients and t-Ratios for PACs in Different Industries

| Industry: | Dependent variables: Percent of budget to | | |
	Democratic incumbents	Republican incumbents	Republican non-incumb.
Mining			
minerals	-1.1 (-0.1)	2.4 (0.7)	-1.3 (-0.3)
coal	5.8 (1.1)	-1.0 (-0.3)	-5.1 (-1.2)
oil & gas	-11.9 (-4.0)	4.2 (1.9)	8.3 (3.3)
Construction	0.3 (0.1)	-2.2 (-0.9)	2.1 (0.7)
Manufacturing			
tobacco	13.9 (1.2)	-11.7 (-1.3)	-2.0 (-0.2)
textiles	-10.3 (-2.1)	1.9 (0.5)	9.0 (2.1)
apparel	-0.9 (-0.1)	3.8 (0.6)	-2.6 (-0.4)
lumber & paper	-4.9 (-1.5)	1.3 (0.5)	4.0 (1.4)
chemicals	-1.7 (-0.7)	2.5 (1.3)	-0.3 (-0.1)
petroleum & coal	-2.7 (-0.7)	-0.9 (-0.3)	4.2 (1.2)
rubber & plastics	-9.3 (-2.9)	0.2 (0.1)	9.3 (3.4)
primary metals	-0.8 (-0.3)	2.2 (1.0)	-1.1 (-0.4)
fabricated metals	-3.9 (-1.3)	2.1 (0.9)	2.7 (1.0)
machinery	-9.6 (-3.4)	1.0 (0.4)	9.0 (3.7)
electrical equip.	-0.2 (-0.1)	1.8 (0.8)	-1.0 (-0.4)
transportation equip.	3.7 (1.2)	0.5 (0.2)	-4.0 (-1.5)
Transportation			
railroads	7.6 (1.5)	-2.8 (-0.7)	-4.6 (-1.0)
local & interurban	8.1 (0.9)	-13.4 (-2.0)	5.9 (0.8)
trucking & warehousing	1.0 (0.2)	0.3 (0.1)	-0.7 (-0.2)
water transportation	18.8 (3.5)	-7.0 (-1.7)	-10.6 (-2.3)
air transportation	5.1 (1.1)	1.1 (0.3)	-5.3 (-1.3)
Utilities	3.8 (1.6)	1.6 (0.9)	-5.5 (-2.7)
Communications	4.5 (1.3)	0.5 (0.2)	-4.5 (-1.6)
Finance			
banking	3.8 (1.6)	-1.9 (-0.9)	-3.3 (-1.4)
credit agencies	9.2 (2.0)	-1.3 (-0.4)	-6.8 (-2.0)
securities	16.5 (3.0)	-11.3 (-2.7)	-5.5 (-1.2)
insurance carriers	4.1 (1.1)	-0.6 (-0.2)	-2.6 (-0.8)
Washington office	13.3 (3.8)	-3.7 (-1.4)	-8.9 (-2.9)
Defense contractor	6.6 (1.9)	1.2 (0.5)	-7.3 (-2.4)
Percent Democratic, homestate delegation	47.7 (9.7)	-52.6 (-14.2)	5.7 (1.4)
Constant	12.6	70.2	14.5
	R^2=.22 N=994	R^2=.21 N=994	R^2=.12 N=994

budgets to Democrats and more to Republican challengers. A most intriguing and instructive case is that of oil PACs, which showed a strong preference for Republican challengers and open seats. On one level this result is not surprising, since it fits with what others have reported about the behavior of oil PACs.[31] On the other hand the oil and gas industry has been the beneficiary of nearly half a century of government largesse through special tax provisions and import quotas. Thus oil's unaccommodating behavior may defy a certain economic logic, but it may also attest to the depth and intensity of business opposition to social regulation, as well as to the oil industry's wrath over what it saw as the Carter administration's betrayal on the issue of natural gas deregulation.[32] Still, when compared to coal and mineral mining, industries with similarly conflicting incentives, the pattern of oil PAC spending is striking indeed.

The partisanship and risk taking of corporate PACs in the 1980 election have not been matched before or since. Even in the 1984 election, with Ronald Reagan and an economic recovery presaging victory for the Republicans, corporate PACs in the aggregate did not venture nearly as great a share of their capital on Republican challengers. Compared to 1980 there was an across-the-board shift away from nonincumbents to incumbents of both parties. However, Table 3.4 shows a remarkable constancy in industry differences. Again, in 1984 support for Democratic incumbents was substantially higher among the PACs of the transportation, communications, utilities, and financial sectors. PACs from sectors of social regulation continued to be less attracted to Democratic officeholders: lumber and paper, textiles, rubber, machinery, and oil remained, on average, less inclined toward incumbent Democrats and generally more inclined toward Republican challengers and open-seat races. Taken together the findings from these two elections provide strong support for the thesis that part of the observed variation in how corporate PACs allocate their funds may be understood by the complex web of government–business relations that has been spun in this century.

Choices between parties and between incumbents and nonincumbents measure only one aspect of the political orientation of corporate PACs. After all, candidates of both political parties come in a great variety of ideological hues. In Table 3.5 we look to see whether there are significant differences across industries in the voting records of the House incumbents supported by corporate PACs in the 1984 election. For this purpose the ratings of Americans for Democratic Action and Americans for Constitutional Action, which are almost mirror images of each other, were taken as crude measures of the ideology of incumbents as expressed in roll call votes. Each of these organizations rates incumbents from zero to one hundred depending on their votes on various litmus tests. The dependent variable in these analyses is the average ADA or ACA rating for the incumbents supported by the PACs in the sample. These ratings, of course, differ markedly from one regional delegation to another. And since we have already seen evidence of the importance of the local connections

Table 3.5
Sectoral Variation in Ideologies of House Incumbent Donees, 1984:
Unstandardized Regression Coefficients and t-Ratios for PACs in Different Industries

Industry:	Dependent variables: Average score of PAC's donees on	
	ADA scale	ACA scale
Mining		
minerals	-3.1 (-1.1)	3.3 (1.3)
coal	1.8 (0.6)	-2.6 (-1.0)
oil & gas	-4.9 (-1.7)	5.0 (1.6)
Construction	-0.6 (-0.3)	-1.0 (-0.5)
Manufacturing		
tobacco	-4.9 (-0.8)	1.8 (0.3)
textiles	0.7 (0.2)	-1.1 (-0.4)
apparel	-1.9 (-0.4)	2.8 (0.7)
lumber & paper	-5.4 (-2.7)	5.4 (3.0)
chemicals	-3.2 (-2.2)	3.4 (2.5)
petroleum & coal	-0.9 (-0.4)	0.9 (0.4)
rubber & plastics	-3.4 (-1.8)	3.5 (2.0)
primary metals	-0.8 (-0.5)	-0.6 (-0.4)
fabricated metals	-2.3 (-1.2)	1.7 (1.0)
machinery	-3.1 (-1.8)	4.3 (2.7)
electrical equip.	-2.4 (-1.4)	2.0 (1.3)
transportation equip.	-1.3 (-0.7)	0.5 (0.3)
Transportation		
railroads	0.2 (0.1)	0.1 (0.1)
local & interurban	2.3 (0.4)	-2.6 (-0.6)
trucking & warehousing	1.0 (0.3)	-1.3 (-0.5)
water transportation	5.9 (1.8)	-7.2 (-2.5)
air transportation	4.5 (1.7)	-5.0 (-2.0)
Utilities	-1.0 (-0.7)	0.7 (0.5)
Communications	5.8 (3.1)	-4.5 (-2.7)
Finance		
banking	5.4 (3.3)	-5.2 (-3.5)
credit agencies	2.3 (1.0)	-2.1 (-1.0)
securities	6.2 (1.9)	-4.0 (-1.4)
insurance carriers	1.1 (0.5)	-1.6 (-0.8)
Defense contractor	0.4 (0.2)	-1.0 (-0.5)
East	3.9 (1.8)	-2.1 (-1.1)
Midwest	-3.8 (-1.8)	5.3 (2.8)
West	-5.6 (-2.5)	7.4 (3.7)
South	-12.3 (-5.8)	10.2 (5.4)
Constant	42.5	48.6
	R^2=.29	R^2=.27
	N=994	N=994

of corporate PACs, we include in the analysis dummy variables for the region in which the PAC is headquartered.[33]

Table 3.5 shows how the average ADA and ACA ratings of donees vary in PACs from different regions and different industries. Regional differences are pronounced. The average ADA scores for the donees of PACs headquartered in the South were sixteen points lower than those for donees of PACs from the East; ACA scores were twelve points higher. PACs in Washington, the average ideology scores of whose donees are measured by the intercept in the regression equation, supported sets of incumbents who were less conservative than those of

Table 3.6
Sectoral Variation in Ideologies of House Democrats, 1984:
Unstandardized Regression Coefficients and t-Ratios for PACs in Different Industries

Industry:	Dependent variables: Average score of PAC's Democratic donees on	
	ADA scale	ACA scale
Mining		
minerals	-2.9 (-0.9)	1.9 (0.8)
coal	4.2 (1.2)	-4.9 (-1.8)
oil & gas	-4.9 (-2.3)	4.1 (2.6)
Construction	-2.9 (-1.1)	1.4 (0.8)
Manufacturing		
tobacco	-8.2 (-1.0)	4.8 (0.8)
textiles	-4.2 (-1.1)	1.1 (0.4)
apparel	-1.2 (-0.2)	2.9 (0.7)
lumber & paper	-4.8 (-2.0)	5.2 (2.9)
chemicals	-2.8 (-1.5)	2.6 (1.9)
petroleum & coal	-2.0 (-0.7)	1.3 (0.6)
rubber & plastics	-3.9 (-1.6)	3.2 (1.8)
primary metals	-2.8 (-1.3)	1.0 (0.6)
fabricated metals	-1.4 (-0.6)	0.3 (0.2)
machinery	-3.0 (-1.4)	3.0 (1.9)
electrical equip.	-3.9 (-1.9)	2.8 (1.8)
transportation equip.	-1.7 (-0.8)	1.1 (0.6)
Transportation		
railroads	0.9 (0.3)	-0.5 (-0.2)
local & interurban	-2.3 (-0.4)	1.6 (0.4)
trucking & warehousing	-0.6 (-0.2)	0.3 (0.1)
water transportation	2.9 (0.8)	-4.0 (-1.4)
air transportation	6.1 (1.8)	-4.3 (-1.8)
Utilities	-2.2 (-1.3)	2.1 (1.7)
Communications	6.5 (2.8)	-4.3 (-2.5)
Finance		
banking	4.4 (2.3)	-3.4 (-2.4)
credit agencies	4.3 (1.6)	-3.0 (-1.5)
securities	6.1 (1.6)	-1.6 (-0.5)
insurance carriers	-2.8 (-1.1)	1.8 (0.9)
Defense contractor	-1.2 (-0.5)	1.0 (0.5)
East	5.4 (2.1)	-3.2 (-1.7)
Midwest	0.8 (0.3)	0.1 (0.1)
West	6.0 (2.0)	-3.6 (-1.8)
South	-16.6 (-6.4)	13.1 (6.9)
Constant	59.4	30.0
	R^2=.34	R^2=.34
	N=906	N=906

all regions outside of the East. The PACs of defense contractors, in contrast, showed no distinctive patterns in the ideologies of their donees.

Standing out along with these differences is the significant variation across industries. By and large PACs from sectors of traditional regulation tended to support incumbents who, on average, were much less conservative than the incumbents supported by PACs from industries affected by social regulation. For example, the average ADA score for donees of banking PACs in the West was forty-two; for PACs from the lumber and paper sector it was thirty. As average differences for all donees, these are substantial indeed.

Of course, the foregoing analysis does not untangle partisanship and ideology, for PACs that gave largely to Republicans would in all likelihood have a set of

Table 3.7
Sectoral Variation in Ideologies of House Republicans, 1984:
Unstandardized Regression Coefficients and t-Ratios for PACs in Different Industries

Industry:	Dependent variables: Average score of PAC's Republican donees on	
	ADA scale	ACA scale
Mining		
minerals	-1.6 (-0.8)	2.1 (1.1)
coal	-0.1 (-0.1)	-0.7 (-0.4)
oil & gas	-1.7 (-1.4)	1.8 (1.5)
Construction	0.8 (0.5)	-1.4 (-1.1)
Manufacturing		
tobacco	-5.0 (-1.1)	3.8 (1.5)
textiles	5.1 (2.3)	-4.2 (-2.0)
apparel	-1.9 (-0.6)	.5 (0.2)
lumber & paper	-0.9 (-0.7)	0.9 (0.7)
chemicals	-1.3 (-1.3)	1.9 (1.9)
petroleum & coal	1.4 (0.8)	-2.0 (-1.2)
rubber & plastics	-0.2 (-0.1)	0.2 (0.1)
primary metals	-0.5 (-0.4)	-0.8 (-0.7)
fabricated metals	-1.2 (-1.0)	0.5 (0.4)
machinery	1.8 (1.4)	-0.4 (-0.3)
electrical equip.	-1.7 (-1.4)	1.3 (1.2)
transportation equip.	-1.3 (-1.0)	0.7 (0.6)
Transportation		
railroads	-0.1 (-0.1)	0.7 (0.3)
local & interurban	4.0 (1.0)	-3.5 (-0.9)
trucking & warehousing	0.5 (0.1)	-1.7 (-0.8)
water transportation	-2.8 (-1.1)	2.2 (1.0)
air transportation	0.1 (0.1)	-3.3 (-1.8)
Utilities	-0.3 (-0.3)	0.9 (0.9)
Communications	3.9 (2.8)	-2.9 (-2.2)
Finance		
banking	2.2 (1.9)	-2.1 (-1.8)
credit agencies	-5.0 (-3.0)	3.9 (2.4)
securities	-0.1 (-0.1)	-0.6 (-0.3)
insurance carriers	-0.2 (-0.1)	0.6 (0.4)
Defense contractor	-0.2 (-0.2)	0.2 (0.1)
East	7.0 (4.4)	-5.5 (-3.7)
Midwest	1.1 (0.7)	0.5 (0.3)
West	-7.2 (-4.4)	8.0 (5.1)
South	-6.4 (-4.1)	7.7 (5.1)
Constant	17.7	74.8
	R^2=.29	R^2=.29
	N=942	N=942

donees who, on average, were more conservative than those of a PAC that gave largely to Democrats. The analyses reported in Tables 3.6 and 3.7 take this into account by separating Republican from Democratic incumbents.[34] Regional effects were again pronounced, with interesting differences between the parties. PACs located in the South and West had sets of Republican donees that were much more conservative than those of other PACs. Such was also the case for Democratic donees of PACs headquartered in the South. PACs located in the West, however, gave to sets of Democratic incumbents who, on average, were more liberal than those of PACs from any other region. This reflects what are sizable interparty differences in the ideologies of the House delegations from the West and, again, the apparent strength of the local connections of corporate PACs.

The differences across industries reported in Tables 3.6 and 3.7 both confirm and add subtlety to our argument about the political orientations of corporate PACs. Even controlling for party there are significant differences from industry to industry in the types of incumbents supported by corporate PACs. By and large, PACs from industries that are the perceived beneficiaries of public policy tend to give to less conservative members of both political parties than those that are the perceived victims of policy. Interestingly, these differences are more muted for Republican donees than for Democratic donees. One reason for this may be that Republican members of the House are somewhat more homogeneous than Democrats. Another reason may have something to do with the realities of institutional power in the House. Thus with Republicans, whose position has been one of a permanent and often feeble minority in the House, corporate PACs of all stripes may feel free to reward conservative position taking. With Democrats, who control the committees and subcommittees important to various industries, ideological considerations confront the hard realities of power. And it is precisely those PACs we would expect—the access seekers of traditionally regulated industries—that appear to be most likely to gravitate toward power rather than purity.

Conclusions

The important choices facing any political action committee are three. How ought funds to be allocated between Republicans and Democrats? How much money ought to be spent on incumbents versus nonincumbents? Ought the PAC lean toward candidates of one ideological stripe or another? The evidence presented in this chapter warrants the conclusion that there is sectoral variation in how PACs make these choices and that this variation can be traced to the diverse experiences of businesses with government. PACs whose parents reside in sectors of traditional economic regulation or who otherwise benefit from public policies tend to pursue narrowly legislative strategies—funneling relatively more resources to Democratic incumbents. Their counterparts in other industries often behave in ways that strongly imply strategies of opposition. PAC dollars from industries that bear the perceived costs of social regulation or other policies flow more heavily into the coffers of Republicans, including challengers and open-seat candidates, and to more conservative members of both parties.

These differences, of course, are matters of degree. Even the most adversarial of PACs are likely to find some incumbents attractive, and the most stalwart Republican partisans are likely to give to at least a few Democrats.[35] This reflects what is in many PACs a tension between accommodation and opposition, a tension with deep roots in American business history. Still, the differences in how this tension plays out in the PACs of various industries are significant, durable, and predictable.

Inattention to the possibility of such differences or for that matter to the rich history of business–government relations in the United States has made the orthodox perspectives on corporate PACs curiously apolitical. From both the progressive and rational-choice perspectives, PACs are bloodless creatures, all of which purchase political power with the same calculations of advantage that they would purchase any other commodity. This is in sharp contrast to the distinctive political colorations of the community of corporate PACs we have found here.

Indeed, in our analysis of the effects of the politics of regulation on campaign finance we have hinted at other ways in which political forces shape the behavior of corporate PACs. To begin with, there is the apparently strong pull that local ties have on these PACs. Standard indictments of political action committees claim that they nationalize campaign finance, investing contributions anywhere they choose in order to maximize their influence and by doing so weakening ties between candidates and their geographic constituencies.[36] Yet here we have seen that much of the variation in how corporate PACs allocate their funds among various types of candidates is traceable to the political circumstances of the states or regions in which the PACs are headquartered. This local connection is examined in detail in Chapter 4.

Analysis of the elections of 1980 and 1984 also revealed that along with consistent differences in PAC strategy across industries there may be across-the-board changes in the behavior of all PACs from one election to another. Thus although the relative position of the industries changed little between 1980 and 1984, there was a general shift in the deployment of PAC money from Republican challengers to Democratic and Republican incumbents. Explaining these occasionally dramatic tactical shifts from election to election requires an understanding of the connections of individual PACs to other political actors, including the national political parties, candidates, and, of course, their own PAC brethren. The outside story of PACs is the subject of Chapter 5.

Notes

1. Arthur Close, ed., *Washington Representatives: Who Does What for Whom in the Nation's Capital?* (Washington, DC: Columbia Press, 1984).

2. Gerald Keim, "Corporate Grassroots Programs in the 1980's," *California Management Review* 28, no. 1 (Fall 1985), pp. 110–23; Mary Ann Pires, "Fertile Fields: The Realization that Politics Starts at Home Has Led to a Harvest of Corporate Grass-Roots Programs," *Public Relations Journal* 42 (November 1986), pp. 36–41.

3. Thomas B. Edsall, *The New Politics of Inequality* (New York: W. W. Norton & Co., 1984), p. 107.

4. Ian Maitland, "Self-Defeating Lobbying: How More Is Buying Less in Washington," *Journal of Business Strategy* 7 (Fall 1986), p. 70.

5. William Lilley and James C. Miller III, "The New Social Regulation," *The Public Interest* 47 (Spring 1977), pp. 49–61; David Vogel, "The 'New' Social Regulation in Historical and Comparative Perspective," in Thomas K. McCaw, ed., *Regulation in Perspective* (Cambridge: Harvard University Press, 1981), pp. 155–86; Paul C. Weaver, "Regulation, Social Policy, and Class Conflict," *The Public Interest* 50 (Winter 1978), pp. 45–63.

6. Eugene Bardach and Robert A. Kagan, eds., *Social Regulation: Strategies for Reform* (San Francisco, CA: Institute for Contemporary Studies, 1982); Stephen Breyer, *Regulation and Its Reform* (Cambridge: Harvard University Press, 1982); Lester B. Lave, *The Strategy of Social Regulation: Decision Frameworks for Policy* (Washington, DC: The Brookings Institution, 1981); Robert E. Litan and William D. Nordhaus, *Reforming Federal Regulation* (New Haven, CT: Yale University Press, 1983); Paul W. MacAvoy, *The Regulated Industries and the Economy* (New York: W. W. Norton and Co., 1979); Charles L. Schultze, *The Public Use of Private Interest* (Washington, DC: The Brookings Institution, 1977); Lawrence J. White, *Reforming Regulation: Processes and Problems* (Englewood Cliffs, NJ: Prentice-Hall, 1981).

7. The complexities of regulatory politics are richly illustrated in the case studies in James Q. Wilson, *The Politics of Regulation* (New York: Basic Books, 1980). See also Kenneth J. Meier, *Regulation: Politics, Bureaucracy, and Economics* (New York: St. Martin's Press, 1985).

8. Wilson, *The Politics of Regulation*, pp. 357–94. Wilson distinguishes the following types of politics: *majoritarian*, where both costs and benefits are widely distributed; *interest-group*, where costs and benefits are both concentrated; *client*, where costs are distributed and benefits concentrated; *entrepreneurial*, where costs are concentrated and benefits distributed.

9. MacAvoy, *The Regulated Industries and the Economy*, p. 88. See also Timothy B. Clark, "How One Company Lives with Government Regulation," *National Journal* (May 12, 1979), pp. 772–79; Lawrence Mosher, "Big Steel Says It Can't Afford to Make the Nation's Air Pure," *National Journal* (July 5, 1980), pp. 1088–92.

10. Litan and Nordhaus, *Reforming Federal Regulation*, p. 26.

11. Wilson, "The Politics of Regulation," p. 370.

12. Thomas K. McCaw, "Regulation in America: A Historical Overview," *California Management Review* 27, no. 1 (Fall 1984), pp. 116–24.

13. MacAvoy, *The Regulated Industries and the Economy*, p. 87. See also Steven Kelman, *Regulating America, Regulating Sweden: A Comparative Study of Occupational Safety and Health Policy* (Cambridge, MA: The MIT Press, 1981); David Vogel, *National Styles of Regulation: Environmental Policy in Great Britain and the United States* (Ithaca, NY: Cornell University Press, 1986).

14. Vogel, "The 'New' Social Regulation in Historical and Comparative Perspective," pp. 164–75.

15. Hugh Heclo and Rudolph G. Penner, "Fiscal and Political Strategy in the Reagan Administration," in Fred I. Greenstein, ed., *The Reagan Presidency* (Baltimore, MD: The Johns Hopkins University Press, 1983), pp. 21–47.

16. A. Grant Jordan, "Iron Triangles, Wooly Corporatism, or Elastic Nets: Images of the Policy Process," *Journal of Public Policy* 1, no. 1 (February 1981), pp. 95–125.

17. Robert A. Leone, *Who Profits* (New York: Basic Books, 1986).

18. Alfred A. Marcus, *The Adversary Economy* (Westport, CT: Quorum Books, 1984); David B. Yoffie and Sigrid Bergenstein, "Creating Political Advantage: The Rise of the Corporate Political Entrepreneur," *California Management Review* 28, no. 1 (Fall 1985), pp. 124–39. For an argument that PAC money and other traditional tools of influence have already substantially weakened social regulations see Susan J. Tolchin and Martin Tolchin, *Dismantling America* (Boston: Houghton Mifflin, 1983).

19. Michael Useem, "The Rise of the Political Manager," *Sloan Management Review* 27 (Fall 1985), pp. 15–26.

20. Edward Handler and John R. Mulkern, *Business in Politics: Campaign Strategies of*

Corporate Political Action Committees (Lexington, MA: Lexington Books, 1982), p. 71. Consider, for example, this description of the PAC of Dow Chemical: "Its PAC is headed up by the director of employee relations and includes a cross representation of different job lines. The company has purposely avoided any feeling that the composition of the policy team was directed from above. It did not decide on the exact form of the policy unit until after the PAC was formed to show employees that it was important for ideas 'to bubble up from the ground and not the other way around.'" Douglas N. Dickson, "CORPACS: The Business of Political Action Committees," *Across the Board* 18 (November 1981), p. 16.

21. James E. Post, Edwin A. Murray, Jr., Robert B. Dickie, and John F. Mahon, "Managing Public Affairs: The Public Affairs Function," *California Management Review* 26, no. 1 (Fall 1983), pp. 135–50.

22. Dickson, "CORPACS: The Business of Political Action Committees," p. 18.

23. Marcus, *The Adversary Economy*, p. 12.

24. On the role of PACs in tax politics see John J. Fialka and Tim Carrington, "The Money Tree: Wall Street's Firms Broaden Gift Lists for Congress Members," *Wall Street Journal* (October 17, 1983), p. 1; Brooks Jackson, "Insurance Industry Boosts Political Contributions as Congress Takes Up Cherished Tax Preferences," *Wall Street Journal* (October 10, 1985), p. 64; Brooks Jackson, "Ways and Means Measure Puts Bigger Tax Bites on Some of the Most Prolific Campaign Donors," *Wall Street Journal* (December 11, 1985), p. 64.

25. Of the 1,067 PACs active in 1980, 685 spent $2,500 or more in House races. In 1984, 994 of the 1,464 active PACs spent $2,500 or more.

26. Not all industries are included in the analysis. However, the industries represented in the sample include those with the most PACs and those that are most relevant to the foregoing discussion of regulatory environments.

27. The data sets used in the analysis were developed from the data files available on the Federal Election Commission's 1979–1980 and 1983–1984 candidate and nonparty committee data tapes. These remarkably detailed files, which summarize the transactions between every candidate and every political action committee in the election cycle, were used to obtain aggregated information about the Standard Industrial Codes of PACs' parent corporations, which was compiled from Marvin Weinberger and David V. Greevy, *The PAC Directory* (Cambridge, MA: Ballinger, 1982). The industry designations used throughout this chapter are defined by the following SIC index numbers: mineral mining, SIC codes 10 and 14; coal mining, 11 and 12; oil and gas extraction, 13; construction, 15, 16, and 17; tobacco manufacturers, 21; textile mill products, 22; apparel, 23; lumber and paper, 24 and 26; chemicals, 28; petroleum and coal products, 29; rubber and plastics, 30; primary metals, 33; fabricated metals, 34; machinery, 35; electrical equipment, 36; transportation equipment, 37; railroad transportation, 40; local and interurban passenger transit, 41; trucking and warehousing, 42; water transportation, 45; communications, 48; utilities, 49; banking, 60; credit agencies, 61; securities and commodities, 62; insurance carriers, 63. For each PAC and industry designation, a value of one was assigned if the PAC resided in that industry; otherwise the PAC was coded zero for that particular code. The dummy variable for Washington location was coded as follows: PAC with an office in Washington was scored one; otherwise the PAC was scored zero. Similarly, PACs representing firms that were among the top fifty

defense contractors were scored one; others were scored zero. Washington PACs were assigned the average score on the variable measuring percentage of the PAC's home state delegation that is Democratic.

28. George A. Thoma, "The Behavior of Corporate Action Committees," *Business and Society* 22 (Spring 1983), pp. 55–58; Marick F. Masters and Gerald D. Keim, "Determinants of PAC Participation Among Large Corporations," *Journal of Politics* 47, no. 4 (November 1985), pp. 1158–73; "Arms Concerns Double Contributions," *New York Times* (April 9, 1985), p. 40.

29. Democratic nonincumbents, for which regressions were not run, received only 1 percent of the House contributions in 1980 and 1984. Separate regressions were also run for Republican challengers and Republican open-seat candidates with results that did not differ materially. For the sake of simplicity these two categories of candidates were collapsed.

30. Willie Schatz, "The Name of the Game Is Now Political Action: Long a 'Sleeping Giant' the Computer Industry Is Now Waking Up to the Importance of PACs," *Datamation* 33 (January 1, 1987), pp. 41–48.

31. David J. Gopoian, "What Makes PACs Tick? An Analysis of the Allocation Patterns of Economic Interest Groups," *American Journal of Political Science* 28 (May 1984), pp. 259–81; Edwin M. Epstein, "PACs and the Modern Political Process," in Betty Bock, Harvey J. Goldschmid, Ira M. Millstein, and F. M. Scherer, eds., *The Impact of the Modern Corporation* (New York: Columbia University Press, 1984), pp. 399–496.

32. On the politics of oil money see Elizabeth Drew, *Politics and Money* (New York: Macmillan, 1983), ch. 7.

33. In the regressions of Tables 3.5 through 3.7 five locations—four geographic regions plus Washington, D.C.—are measured by these dummy variables: EAST, PACs located in Connecticut, Delaware, Maine, Maryland, Massachusetts, New Hampshire, New Jersey, New York, Pennsylvania, Rhode Island or Vermont; MIDWEST, Illinois, Indiana, Iowa Kansas, Michigan, Minnesota, Missouri, Nebraska, North Dakota, Ohio, South Dakota, or Wisconsin; WEST, Alaska, Arizona, California, Colorado, Hawaii, Idaho, Montana, Nevada, New Mexico, Oregon, Utah, Washington, or Wyoming; SOUTH, Alabama, Arkansas, Florida, Georgia, Kentucky, Louisiana, Mississippi, North Carolina, Oklahoma, South Carolina, Tennessee, Texas, Virginia, or West Virginia. Each PAC was coded with the value of one for its region and zero on all other regional dummies. The average ideologies of donees for PACs based in Washington, D.C. are measured by the intercepts of the regressions.

34. There were some PACs that did not give to any Democratic incumbents and others that did not give to any Republican incumbents. This accounts for the slightly smaller number of cases in these regressions as well as the difference in the number of cases in the Republican and Democratic regressions.

35. It is not uncommon for PACs to give to the incumbent and the challenger in the same race. For examples see "Business 'Double Dips' for Candidates," *Business Week* (August 16, 1982), p. 113.

36. Amitai Etzioni, *Capital Corruption* (New York: Harcourt Brace Jovanovich, 1984).

4

The Political Geography of Corporate PACs

Corporate political action committees all claim a common institutional parent-
age, but they vary in virtually every other way—in their financial strength, in
the number of candidates they support, in their basic strategies for contributing,
in their responses to government regulation. The basic outlines of the first of
these, budget size, were described in Chapter 2. In both 1980 and 1984 we
encountered a wide range of budgets among corporate committees. About a
third spent less than $2,500; but one PAC in four made direct contributions of
$15,000 or more, and the rest were scattered haphazardly in between. Of course,
these differences may be interesting in themselves, but do they really matter? Do
PACs become more "innovative" as they grow, perhaps allotting more support
to nonincumbents? Or is the acceptance of risk characteristic of the PAC dwarf
with little to lose? Does size foster bureaucratization, a diminished willingness to
take chances? Or do large PACs tend to "diversify" their political investments?
Obviously, since we have before us a large class of organizations that vary
substantially in size, we can address some interesting questions about the effects
of slack resources and professionalization on organizational behavior.

Yet when it comes to PACs the analysis of size is not quite so straightforward.
Empirical questions about their financial clout are difficult to untangle from the
larger issue of where PACs fit within the democratic fabric of American politics.
We can trace this difficulty to a tenet of the American reform tradition—that as
the political treasuries of private interests grow more formidable, the accountability of those in charge begins to weaken and the threat to democratic representation begins to loom large. PACs rarely have formal mechanisms ensuring
that decision makers answer to donors for their actions. And though in this
respect they are virtually indistinguishable from most staff organizations, questions of internal responsibility have dogged political action committees. As

Frank J. Sorauf suggests, such questions persist for PACs "partly because of the widespread belief that group leadership is often unrepresentative of the group membership."[1] A corollary belief is this: The problem of accountability increases with the size of the PAC.

Another worry is that political action committees, by creating large pools of unaccountable money, help to detach members of Congress from their local constituencies. Localism, for some, is a moral imperative of American political life:

Table 4.1
PAC Size and Contributory Behavior:
Percentage of PACs of Different Budget Sizes Allocating
Specified Proportions to Three Types of House Candidates, 1980

Percent of Total Spent on Candidate Type:	Total Contributions in Dollars (Number of PACs)						
	0–2500 (372)	2501–5000 (184)	5001–7500 (108)	7501–10000 (64)	10001–15000 (101)	15001–Above (238)	All (1067)
Democratic Incumbents							
0.0 to 20.0	40.6%	29.4%	24.1%	34.4%	33.7%	25.6%	32.6%
20.1 to 50.0	29.3	37.0	40.7	32.8	35.6	43.3	35.7
50.1 to 79.9	14.3	26.1	30.6	26.6	27.7	29.0	23.2
80.0 to 100.0	15.9	7.6	4.6	6.3	3.0	2.1	8.4
Totals*	100.1%	100.0%	100.0%	100.1%	100.0%	100.0%	99.9%
Republican Incumbents							
0.0 to 20.0	48.4%	37.5%	29.6%	18.8%	25.7%	12.6%	32.7%
20.1 to 50.0	29.3	51.1	53.7	65.6	58.4	79.8	51.7
50.1 to 79.9	12.9	10.9	16.7	15.6	15.8	7.6	12.2
80.0 to 100.0	9.4	0.5	0.0	0.0	0.0	0.0	3.4
Totals*	100.0%	100.0%	100.0%	100.0%	99.9%	100.0%	99.9%
Republican Non-Incumbents							
0.0 to 20.0	50.5%	46.2%	51.9%	46.9%	42.6%	43.3%	47.3%
20.1 to 50.0	27.2	29.9	32.4	35.9	38.6	42.4	33.2
50.1 to 79.9	11.6	16.9	11.1	15.6	14.9	12.6	13.2
80.0 to 100.0	10.8	7.1	4.6	1.6	4.0	1.7	6.3
Totals*	100.1%	100.1%	100.0%	100.0%	100.1%	100.0%	100.0%

*Columns may not sum to 100.0% due to rounding error.

The evidence is overwhelming that the power of PACs, reaching across state and district lines, erodes the very essence of representational government.... There is now more than ever a sordid image of many of our legislators thinking more of money sources than of their constituents, of legislators lobbying PACs to be be elected, and then, expressly or subliminally, factoring this into their voting decisions when, after their election, the PACs lobby them.[2]

Table 4.2
PAC Size and Contributory Behavior:
Percentage of PACs of Different Budget Sizes Allocating
Specified Proportions to Three Types of House Candidates, 1984

Percent of Total Spent on Candidate Type:	Total Contributions in Dollars (Number of PACs)						
	0-2500 (469)	2501-5000 (228)	5001-7500 (123)	7501-10000 (99)	10001-15000 (131)	15001-Above (414)	All (1464)
Democratic Incumbents							
0.0 to 20.0	42.2%	24.6%	26.8%	28.3%	21.4%	16.4%	28.1%
20.1 to 50.0	20.3	30.7	37.4	32.3	38.2	42.0	31.9
50.1 to 79.9	13.7	30.7	30.9	26.3	34.4	39.4	27.7
80.0 to 100.0	23.9	14.0	4.9	13.1	6.1	2.2	12.3
Totals*	100.1%	100.0%	100.0%	100.0%	100.1%	100.0%	100.0%
Republican Incumbents							
0.0 to 20.0	41.4%	29.8%	22.0%	27.3%	16.0%	7.0%	25.0%
20.1 to 50.0	22.8	41.2	50.4	47.5	54.2	73.2	46.7
50.1 to 79.9	14.7	22.4	24.4	22.2	28.2	19.8	19.9
80.0 to 100.0	21.1	6.6	3.3	3.0	1.5	0.0	8.4
Totals*	100.0%	100.0%	100.1%	100.0%	99.9%	100.0%	100.0%
Republican Non-Incumbents							
0.0 to 20.0	72.1%	70.2%	61.0%	59.6%	65.7%	67.9%	68.2%
20.1 to 50.0	17.1	20.6	27.6	28.3	24.4	25.6	22.3
50.1 to 79.9	5.5	7.0	8.1	9.1	8.4	5.8	6.6
80.0 to 100.0	5.3	2.2	3.3	3.0	1.5	0.7	2.9
Totals*	100.0%	100.0%	100.0%	100.0%	100.0%	100.0%	100.0%

*Columns may not sum to 100.0% due to rounding error.

Beneath the evocative prose lie two related empirical claims. First, political action committees have functional interests that are naturally incompatible with the interests of electoral constituencies. Second, in contrast to the parochialism of campaign supporters within states and districts, PACs are cosmopolitan contributors, shrewdly investing substantial resources in auspicious races beyond their home state boundaries. Again, such incompatibilities can only worsen as PAC resources grow. With growth comes centralization, and inescapably these "nationally centralized institutions...compete with local constituents...for the attention of public officials."[3]

We know that out-of-state PAC donations comprise an ample proportion of the typical campaign war chest, at least for Senate candidates running in smaller states.[4] Clearly, if the same is true for political action committees—that is, if the typical PAC views the electoral fates of out-of-state candidates as vital enough to warrant serious budgetary attention—then successful office seekers indeed may be obliged to "weigh the interests of their own constituents with those of their financial constituents across the country."[5] The issue of representation is an important one, and we will look for evidence of provincialism and sophistication in the contributions of corporate committees. But first we return to the question that introduced this chapter: Do big PACs and small PACs behave in different ways?

PAC Size and Strategies of Contribution

Tables 4.1 and 4.2, which report the 1980 and 1984 contribution profiles for PACs of different sizes, provide an answer. These figures again affirm a familiar caveat: The "average" corporate PAC, as described by the aggregate data, simply does not exist. The right-most columns of Tables 4.1 and 4.2 recall the overall patterns discussed in Chapter 2. For example, in 1980 about a third of all active corporate committees allotted 20 percent or less to Democratic incumbents; roughly a third gave moderate amounts of 20 to 50 percent; and a third contributed better than half their budgets to Democratic officeholders. But these figures are not reliable guideposts for the spending habits of committees in any of the size categories. PACs with limited budgets are much more specialized in their candidate preferences and are thus more polarized as a group. In 1984, for instance, over 40 percent of the smallest class allotted low proportions (20 percent or less) to Democratic incumbents, but practically one-quarter gave heavy allocations. Interestingly, this pattern for small PACs is reminiscent of the aggregated profile of nonconnected committees, which tend as individual organizations to show singular devotion to either Democrats or Republicans.[6] The larger corporate PACs, by contrast, appear more catholic in their giving, clustering in the middle ranges of proportionate support in both years. This holds for all three candidate types, although corporate PAC support for Republican nonincumbents is somewhat less differentiated on the basis of budget size. By and large, however, if we were to dub as a "specialist" any committee that contributes at least 80 percent of its budget to one type of candidate, then in 1980 the label applies to one PAC dwarf in three (in 1984 better than one in two), but it fits barely one-tenth of the corporate PACs that spent more than $10 thousand in each year.

What accounts for this distinctive specialization-to-diversification gradient between dwarfs and giants? Is this difference mainly a function of size? Indeed, PACs with few assets would have scarcely enough to meet basic priorities. Or perhaps the chief reason for the committee's creation—to provide visible if token support for a handful of candidates—was modest from the start. In any event, basic priorities and chief reasons probably forge unalloyed strategies— Democratic or Republican accommodation in both years, and (in 1980 anyway) purer tactics of opposition. As the number of dollars expands so do the opportunities for mixed strategies.

Yet there may be more going on here than meets the eye, for we know that the size of a PAC's treasury is related to other important organizational forces. Large PACs, for example, are more likely to maintain key Washington contacts, and committee decision makers will enjoy a good measure of discretion. A Potomac point of view may counsel pragmatism as well as strategic diversity. And small PACs are not just small; they tend to be located in the political hinterland, far from the more sophisticated world of Beltway politics. The blandishments of local candidates, the importuning of party officials, the demands of a bothersome donor or chief executive officer—any one of these could commit an entire contribution budget for a PAC with meager resources. Clearly, a richer understanding of PAC behavior requires an appreciation for *where* they are, not simply *how much* they have to spend.

The Political Geography of Corporate PACs

Figure 4.1 shows the geographical distribution of all corporate PACs that made direct contributions to House candidates in the 1984 general elections. It is plain to see that corporate political action committees are indeed a far-flung lot. Virtually every state served as home base for these organizations in 1984, and with predictable concentrations—ranging from a solitary PAC in West Virginia to 156 in the state of Texas. Table 4.3, which totals the contributions for each state's PACs and reports the proportion given to home state candidates, lends additional depth and perspective. As one might expect, the largest states boast the most PACs and account for the bulk of the spending. Committees headquartered in just six states—California, Illinois, New York, Ohio, Pennsylvania, and Texas—together contributed $12 million to House campaigns in 1984. Add to this the $1.6 million from PACs based in the District of Columbia, and we can account for over half of the money contributed by all corporate committees during the election cycle.

If corporate PACs display diversity in their geographic origins, so too do they distribute their resources with divergent degrees of respect for home state

Figure 4.1
The Political Geography of Political Action Committees:
Number of PACs Located in Each State, 1984

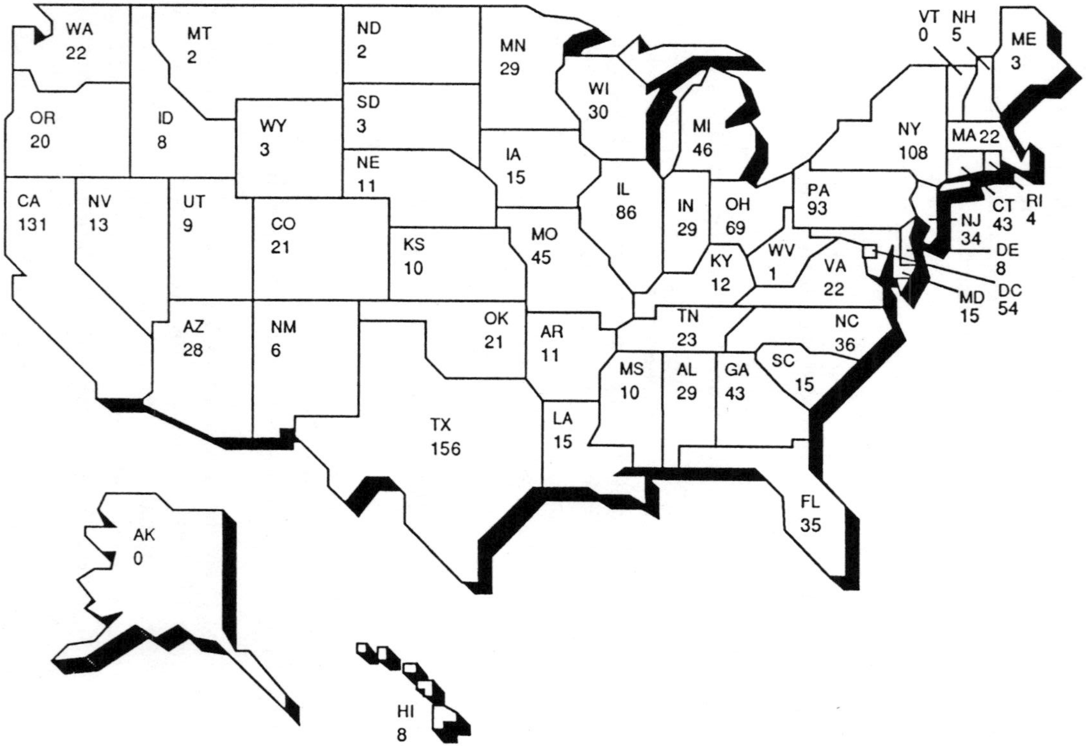

Table 4.3
Corporate PACs State-by-State: Total Contributions and
Percentage of Contributions Spent In-State, 1984 House Elections

State	Total $	% Spent In-State	State	Total $	% Spent In-State
Alabama	$ 380,830	41.6%	Nebraska	$ 116,110	26.4%
Arizona	137,465	47.9	Nevada	57,670	76.4
Arkansas	42,390	22.7	New Hampshire	66,800	12.0
California	2,940,738	32.5	New Jersey	682,423	20.0
Colorado	196,807	33.9	New Mexico	13,055	86.0
Connecticut	981,151	8.3	New York	2,883,285	17.8
Delaware	99,072	4.6	N. Carolina	471,920	34.9
Florida	756,971	30.7	N. Dakota	2,150	19.8
Georgia	427,288	42.0	Ohio	1,008,591	22.3
Hawaii	20,786	92.5	Oklahoma	292,325	13.6
Idaho	54,200	18.5	Oregon	160,438	39.0
Illinois	1,612,354	23.9	Pennsylvania	1,169,808	27.2
Indiana	273,338	37.0	Rhode Island	78,785	5.8
Iowa	91,740	73.8	S. Carolina	69,870	73.1
Kansas	108,912	12.2	S. Dakota	3,335	95.8
Kentucky	183,755	14.3	Tennessee	342,281	25.3
Louisiana	152,050	36.3	Texas	2,347,497	39.6
Maine	9,200	94.6	Utah	40,965	59.5
Maryland	259,646	15.5	Virginia	262,948	23.0
Massachusetts	235,953	34.8	Washington	276,122	34.0
Michigan	785,739	23.9	W. Virginia	13,100	19.5
Minnesota	315,001	30.7	Wisconsin	176,106	37.7
Mississippi	28,350	65.6	Wyoming	4,550	7.7
Missouri	765,784	24.6	Wash., D. C.	1,624,094	
Montana	10,330	14.4			
			All PACs	$23,033,978	25.8%

boundaries. All told, of the $23 million they gave to House candidates in 1984, corporate PACs allotted some $5.9 million, about 26 percent, to candidates from their home states.[7] But of course this aggregate amount glosses over a lot of state-to-state variation. The range of this variation is wide, from less than 5 percent for PACs headquartered in Delaware to over 95 percent for PACs in South Dakota. These state-level numbers prefigure an important fact: There is a good deal of local spending by many individual corporate PACs. Beyond this, it appears that the proportions for the largest states are lower and less erratic (Texas PACs are high with some 40 percent of their money ending up in-state), suggesting another question worth pursuing for individual committees: At what point do big PACs run out of home state opportunities and look elsewhere for candidates to support?

Table 4.4
Corporate PAC Support for Home State Candidates:
Percentage of PACs Allocating Specified Proportions of Their Budgets to
In-State Races, and Dollar Amounts Spent, 1980 and 1984

Proportion of a PAC's Budget Allocated to In-State Races, From % To %		Distribution of PACs and Dollars			
		1980		1984	
From %	To %	PACs (N=1067)	Dollars (x 1000)	PACs (N=1464)	Dollars (x 1000)
0	0	3.7%	$ 70	5.6%	$ 324
.1	24.9	26.3	6437	25.6	13242
25.0	49.9	17.6	2546	14.9	3862
50.0	74.9	11.7	826	13.5	1895
75.0	99.9	14.5	857	12.2	1311
100.0	100.0	23.2	496	24.5	776
Washington PACs		2.9	596	3.7	1624
Totals*		99.9%	$11828	100.0%	$23034

*Columns may not sum to 100.0% due to rounding error.

To get a better idea of how much home state spending goes on at the level of individual political action committees, we categorized non-Washington PACs based on the proportion of their total budgets they devoted to in-state candidates, from 0 percent through 100 percent. Table 4.4 reports the distributions of PACs for 1980 and 1984. (To provide a complete profile we include Washington-based committees as a separate class, plus the gross dollar amounts contributed by PACs in each category.) These figures reveal a surprising amount of local spending. In both elections half of all committees contributed at least half of their budgets to home state candidates. In fact, practically one committee in four spent all of its money at home, while an insignificant handful contributed exclusively to races being staged elsewhere. To be sure, we do not encounter large dollar amounts in the higher ranges of local giving: the total spending of PACs allocating at least half of their money in-state represents less than 20 percent of all PAC contributions in each year. However, we do encounter a large number of political action committees. Clearly, if races close to home are this important to so many PACs, it is little wonder that state-to-state differences in contributory opportunities account for much of the variation in the spending behavior of corporate committees. Thus the makeup of a PAC's home state delegation, as reported in the regressions of Chapter 3, is strongly related to budgetary allotments.

Furthermore, the tendency to forsake in-state candidacies seems to develop rather slowly as PAC resources grow. In Tables 4.5 and 4.6 we show how corporate committees of different budget sizes distributed themselves across our

Table 4.5
PAC Size and Support for Home State Candidates:
In-State Allocations for PACs of Different Budget Sizes, 1980

Percent of Total Spent In-State	Total Contributions in Dollars						
	0-2500	2501-5000	5001-7500	7501-10000	10001-15000	15001-Above	Totals
0 percent	7.5% (28)	4.4% (8)	2.8% (3)	0.0% (0)	0.0% (0)	0.0% (0)	3.7% (39)
.1 to 24.9	4.3 (16)	16.3 (30)	20.4 (22)	40.6 (26)	38.6 (39)	62.2 (148)	26.3 (281)
25.0 to 49.9	9.4 (35)	17.9 (33)	26.9 (29)	21.9 (14)	23.8 (24)	22.3 (53)	17.6 (188)
50.0 to 74.9	11.6 (43)	16.3 (30)	11.1 (12)	17.2 (11)	16.8 (17)	5.0 (12)	11.7 (125)
75.0 to 99.9	14.8 (55)	22.8 (42)	25.0 (27)	10.9 (7)	15.8 (16)	3.4 (8)	14.5 (155)
100 percent	50.8 (189)	21.2 (39)	12.0 (13)	7.8 (5)	0.0 (0)	.8 (2)	23.2 (248)
Washington PACs	1.6 (6)	1.1 (2)	1.9 (2)	1.6 (1)	5.0 (5)	6.3 (15)	2.9 (31)
Totals*	100.0% (372)	100.0% (184)	99.9% (108)	100.0% (64)	100.0% (101)	100.0% (238)	99.9% (1067)

*Columns may not sum to 100.0% due to rounding error.

Table 4.6
PAC Size and Support for Home State Candidates:
In-State Allocations for PACs of Different Budget Sizes, 1984

Percent of Total Spent In-State	Total Contributions in Dollars						
	0-2500	2501-5000	5001-7500	7501-10000	10001-15000	15001-Above	Totals
0 percent	11.7% (55)	5.3% (12)	1.6% (2)	1.0% (1)	4.6% (6)	1.5% (6)	5.6% (82)
.1 to 24.9	4.9 (23)	12.3 (28)	19.5 (24)	18.2 (18)	32.1 (42)	57.7 (239)	25.6 (374)
25.0 to 49.9	6.0 (28)	17.5 (40)	13.8 (17)	16.2 (16)	24.4 (32)	20.5 (85)	14.9 (218)
50.0 to 74.9	9.6 (45)	16.7 (38)	27.6 (34)	24.2 (24)	16.8 (22)	8.5 (35)	13.5 (198)
75.0 to 99.9	9.0 (42)	21.9 (50)	25.2 (31)	21.2 (21)	13.0 (17)	4.4 (18)	12.2 (179)
100 percent	57.0 (267)	24.6 (56)	10.6 (13)	14.1 (14)	5.3 (7)	.5 (2)	24.5 (359)
Washington PACs	1.9 (9)	1.8 (4)	1.6 (2)	5.1 (5)	3.8 (5)	7.0 (29)	3.7 (54)
Totals*	100.1% (469)	100.1% (228)	99.9% (123)	100.0% (99)	100.0% (131)	100.1% (414)	100.0% (1464)

measure of in-state contributions in 1980 and 1984. (The right-hand marginals of these two cross tabulations restate the simple percentage distributions of Table 4.4.) Apparently, as treasuries expand and home state opportunities are depleted, PACs begin to look elsewhere, or tend to *be* elsewhere—in Washington, D.C. While over half of the smaller PACs in the left-most columns of Table 4.5 and Table 4.6 expended their meager budgets at home, some 60 percent of the best-endowed group gave less than twenty-five cents of each contribution dollar to in-state candidates. And in both years Washington PACs, not surprisingly, are overrepresented among the well-to-do. Yet between these two poles a gently sloping curve would serve to capture the relationship, for PACs apparently do not scramble for out-of-state races as campaign money becomes more plentiful. From the right-hand marginals we can see that over 35 percent of corporate PACs in both 1980 and 1984 spent at least 75 percent of their budgets in-state. This figure provides a fairly durable benchmark; only as contributions grow toward the ten thousand dollar mark does this heavy in-state commitment begin to disappear. Fully one-third of the PACs in the respectable ten to fifteen thousand dollar range still disbursed half their money to home state connections.

The Local Connection: A Closer Look

What is it about home state territory that apparently exerts such a strong pull on so many committees? Are these forces distinctive enough to be revealed by a comparison of PACs' in-state and out-of-state spending? In answering these questions one can entertain two conflicting yet equally plausible expectations. We might expect the familiar "two Congresses" phenomenon to apply to PACs as well as voters.[8] That is to say, a PAC may be more satisfied with the performance of its home state officeholders than with Congress as an institution. And this might produce in-state giving with an accommodationist flavor, with more generous allotments for incumbents, especially Democratic incumbents. Contributions deployed elsewhere, by this view, would betray partisan or adversarial motivations. Out-of-state Republicans—especially nonincumbent Republicans—would benefit from this disparity. On the other hand, most corporate PACs are simply not privy to the incumbent-centered game of Washington politics, and they may be more receptive to the overtures of state party organizations and geographically closer to the pleas of local challengers. Indeed, as we argued in Chapter 2, the world of the local corporate committee can be a strongly ideological one.

In order to sort out these different expectations, we first divided the total spending of each corporate PAC into two separate budgets: contributions given in-state and contributions given out-of-state. (Obviously, Washington PACs and PACs spending all their money either in-state or out-of-state were not included in this part of our analysis.) We then calculated the proportions of each of these amounts allocated to Democratic incumbents, Republican incumbents,

Table 4.7
In-State and Out-of-State Spending Compared:
Percentage of PACs Allocating Specified Proportions of
Their In-State and Out-of-State Contributions
to Three Types of Candidates, 1980 and 1984

Candidate Type	Percent of Contributions					
	0.0-19.9	20.0-39.9	40.0-59.9	60.0-79.9	80.0-100.0	Totals*
PACs, by In-State Spending, 1980						
Dem. Incumb.	43.7	16.0	19.4	10.3	10.7	100.1%
Rep. Incumb.	38.2	23.0	19.0	12.0	7.9	100.1%
Rep. Non-Inc.	47.7	19.8	13.9	9.6	9.1	100.1%
PACs, by Out-of-State Spending, 1980						
Dem. Incumb.	33.6	20.0	19.2	13.6	13.5	99.9%
Rep. Incumb.	31.4	38.7	19.1	3.3	7.5	100.0%
Rep. Non-Inc.	52.7	18.4	15.8	7.2	5.9	100.0%
PACs, by In-State Spending, 1984						
Dem. Incumb.	36.5	16.9	19.4	14.2	12.9	99.9%
Rep. Incumb.	28.6	21.3	25.3	13.1	11.8	100.1%
Rep. Non-Inc.	64.8	15.3	8.8	4.5	6.6	100.0%
PACs, by Out-of-State Spending, 1984						
Dem. Incumb.	27.9	19.9	21.1	14.8	16.4	100.1%
Rep. Incumb.	25.8	30.7	27.6	8.4	7.6	100.1%
Rep. Non-Inc.	70.1	14.6	7.5	3.4	4.4	100.0%

Note: For 1980, N=749; for 1984, N=969.
*Rows may not sum to 100.0% due to rounding error.

and Republican nonincumbents. Table 4.7 shows the relevant distributions for corporate PACs in 1980 and 1984.

These figures suggest that at-home contributions are more likely to end up in the war chests of Republican incumbents and nonincumbents than is money spent elsewhere. And Democratic incumbents, certainly not neglected as members of the home state congressional class, enjoy even greater budgetary attention if they hail from out-of-state. In 1980, for example, about one PAC in five gave large proportional amounts (over 60 percent) of their in-state budgets to Democratic officeholders. Yet this differs very little from the support given to home state GOP incumbents and nonincumbents: about 20 percent of all committees contributed at least 60 percent of their in-state budgets to Republican incumbents, and only slightly less than 20 percent gave at least 60 percent to Republican outsiders. Indeed the distributions across the first three rows of Table 4.7 are remarkably alike. This symmetry disappears for out-of-state contributions. Here the center of gravity shifts sharply toward Democratic accommodation: better than one PAC in four gave at least 60 percent of its budget to Democratic incumbents; barely one in ten showed commensurate support for Republican candidates of either stripe. The penchant for in-state Republicans and out-of-state Democrats shows up in 1984 as well, despite aggregate changes in the behavior of corporate PACs.

Thus different consellations of forces may be at work inside and outside state boundaries. Beholden to the home district incumbent who helped fight some battle with the bureaucracy, or prudently obliged to consider some future corporate need, political action committees certainly are not immune to pragmatic considerations in disbursing their in-state money. However, when freed from such local concerns, and freed as well from within-state restrictions on their contributory opportunities, corporate PACs tilt even more strongly toward Democratic incumbents. Conversely, the signs of Republican partisanship and adversarialism, which at least are traceable in-state, fade noticeably in the out-of-state spending profile. This suggests that the partisan cues PAC decision makers receive—from persuasive state-level GOP professionals, from desperate yet sympathetic Republican nonincumbents—have their intended home state effects. And our data clearly support Edward Handler and John R. Mulkern's argument that ideological and partisan appeals, while they may help PAC organizers raise money within the ranks of middle and upper management, might also foster expectations that constrain the most visible spending decisions committee leaders must make.[9]

Indeed, when we compare PACs that are insulated from state and local pressures with PACs that are more susceptible to such forces, we see a caricature of the above patterns. Table 4.8 reports the overall spending behavior for committees that gave exclusively to in-state candidates—we call them "parochial PACs"—and the overall spending of PACs based in Washington, D.C. To account for within-state spending opportunities, each parochial PAC was placed into one of three subgroups, based on the partisan composition of its congressional delegation. (For example, the top row of Table 4.8 shows the combined 1980 contribution profile for all parochial PACs from states having heavy Democratic representation in the House. The second row provides the same information for committees residing in states with a split delegation, and the third for parochial PACs from heavily Republican states.) These subgroups define the most predictable yet least revealing feature of the data: When faced with a candidate field populated mostly by Democratic incumbents seeking reelection, parochial PAC dollars flowed heavily to these officeholders and to their opponents. As a group, PACs in Democratic states gave slightly less than

Table 4.8
Parochial PACs and Washington PACs Compared:
Percentage Distribution of Total Contributions to Four Types of Candidates,
by Makeup of Home State Delegation, 1980 and 1984

Parochial PAC's House Delegation is:*	Percentage Distribution of Total Contributions				
	Democratic		Republican		
	Inc.	Non-Inc.	Inc.	Non-Inc.	Totals**
Parochial PACs, 1980					
Democratic	47.5%	8.3	13.9	30.3	100.0%
Split	35.9%	3.4	38.5	22.2	100.0%
Republican	18.7%	16.1	31.1	34.1	100.0%
Parochial PACs, 1984					
Democratic	44.6%	3.4	22.6	29.4	100.0%
Split	25.9%	5.4	50.9	17.8	100.0%
Republican	9.7%	0.2	61.9	28.2	100.0%
Washington PACs, 1980					
	44.7%	1.1	34.0	20.1	99.9%
Washington PACs, 1984					
	50.4%	1.1	37.3	11.2	100.0%

*State delegations comprised of over 60.0% Democrats are "Democratic," those between 40.1% and 60.0% are "split," and those with 40.0% or fewer Democrats are "Republican."

**Rows may not sum to 100.0% due to rounding error.

Note: For 1980, N=31 for Washington PACs; N=248 for parochial PACs, 110 of which have "Democratic" delegations, 112 "split," and 26 "Republican." For 1984, N=54 for Washington PACs; N=359 for parochial PACs, 190 "Democratic," 125 "split," and 44 "Republican."

half of their contributions (47.5 percent in 1980 and 44.6 percent in 1984) to Democratic incumbents and slightly less than a third (30.3 percent and 29.4 percent) to Republican nonincumbents. But Republican incumbents were never shunned—even in predominantly Democratic states—and support for GOP outsiders remained strong across all partisan environments. Indeed, as the incumbent field became more competitive and finally more Republican, parochial PACs deserted the Democrats with astonishing speed, yet their allotments to Republican nonincumbents barely wavered. (The 1980 receipts of Republican nonincumbents in Republican states were *greater* than those of any other candidate type.)

The partisan pull of in-state Republican forces becomes even more evident when we consider the modal behavior of corporate committees. The figures in

Table 4.8 for Washington PACs reflect the national trend: Republican non-incumbents, who as a class received generous support in 1980, were unceremoniously abandoned in favor of incumbents, especially Democrats, in 1984. In fact, of all corporate contributions to House races in 1980, about 30 percent went to Republican nonincumbents; in 1984, barely more than 15 percent.[10] Viewed in this light, the spending behavior of parochial PACs is perversely counter-cyclical. These groups grew even more ardently pro-Republican in 1984. To be sure, GOP incumbents were the chief beneficiaries of this. But the other trend in the national tide, the shift toward Democrats, was stiffly resisted by these small PACs from the political periphery.

Of course, for the many corporate committees that spend most of the money—say, those allotting less than half their budgets in-state—there is a more subtle balance between the pro-Republican sentiments of the home office and the accommodationist logic of corporate legislative designs. Even so, our findings so far point the same way as previous evidence: organizations that count on the efforts of faraway confederates to build sizable centralized treasuries can count on something else as well—parochial demands will surely intrude upon and shape strategy.[11] Thus one could speculate that without local outlets for partisanship and adversarialism, nationalized corporate PACs are likely to become conduits for those motivations. A concluding look at a subset of our data reinforces this suspicion.

Table 4.9
Two Types of Washington PACs Compared:
Basic Contribution Strategies for the Largest Corporate PACs
with and without Affiliates, 1984 House Elections

		Percentage Distribution of Total Contributions				
		Democratic		Republican		Totals*
		Inc.	Non-Inc.	Inc.	Non-Inc.	
		Washington PACs				
With Affiliates (N=6)	%	56.1%	.7	36.6	6.6	100.0% $313,400
Without Affiliates (N=11)	%	40.7%	1.4	42.5	15.4	100.0% $713,415
		Non-Washington PACs				
With Washington Affiliate (N=13)	%	46.8%	2.7	37.2	13.4	100.1% $130,320
Without Affiliates (N=135)	%	41.6%	1.2	40.0	17.1	99.9% $8,946,115

*Rows may not sum to 100.0% due to rounding error.

Table 4.9, which is based on the 1984 spending behavior of the largest corporate PACs, allows some simple comparisons between Washington committees with different organizational arrangements.[12] The corporate PACs in the first row are nationally based, but they have active non-Washington affiliates, which typically are located with the corporation's home office and its various divisions. (The spending behavior of these affiliates is shown in the third row of Table 4.9.) Similarly, the Washington PACs in the second row have corporate parents who reside elsewhere, but these committees are the only PACs sponsored by their firms. Finally, the most numerous species of corporate committees, the non-Washington PAC without affiliates, occupies the last row of Table 4.9.

Washington-based corporate committees are quite rare to begin with. And only about a third of them, albeit the richest third, appear in this subset of our data. (These seventeen PACs spent over $1 million, which represents nearly two-thirds of the contributions made by all Washington corporate PACs in 1984.) In any case, the two sorts of nationalized committees deployed their resources in dramatically different ways. Washington PACs with affiliates show the strongest support for Democratic incumbents and among the lowest levels of Republican giving we have yet reported. And this occurred during a year in which Washington PACs as a group soared to new heights of Democratic accommodation. As Table 4.8 shows, in 1984, 88 percent of their contribution dollars were given to incumbents, half to Democratic officeholders. Yet half was not enough for the Washington affiliates of Table 4.9. Well over 90 percent of their $300 thousand in contributions went to insiders, and this generosity was not directed toward the Republican side of the aisle. Washington committees without affiliates, by contrast, barely lived up to the new standard of Democratic patronage. Indeed they would appear in 1984 to be fighting the same battles as our garden-variety corporate PAC, the non-Washington committee without affiliates: a more pro-Republican cast to incumbent-bound dollars, a pro-GOP pull for nonincumbent contributions. Again this evidence is consistent with what others have said about the effects of local organizational pressures on national decision makers. And it is consistent as well with what we have found, in the case of corporate PACs, to be the strongly partisan direction of those pressures.

Conclusion

The internal lives of corporate PACs are elusive, and the instruments we have for looking inside are crude and roundabout. Much of the direct evidence about their organizational politics, such as interviews with PAC managers and surveys of PAC donors, comes from the most visible and accessible committees, many of which are headquartered in Washington.[13] By now it should be clear that the leaders of the largest and most centrally located PACs do not inhabit the same world as the managers of most committees.

Perhaps we have referred too frequently to the different "worlds" of corporate PACs, but it is hard to think of a more suitable metaphor for capturing what we have found and recounted here. Of course an important quantitative metric, budget size, appears to be an influential arbiter of contributory style— more money brings greater flexibility—but the qualitative differences between PACs emerge as most prominent in our investigation. The phenomenon of in-state giving especially adds texture to our unfolding portrait of corporate PACs. To be sure, the popular stereotype of the free-spending, nationalized giant has a clear empirical referent here. After all, though they accounted for less than 4 percent of all active committees in 1984, Washington PACs alone were responsible for some 7 percent of all direct contributions. And among non-Washington committees the bulk of the 1984 contribution dollars (about 60 percent) came from PACs that allocated less than one-quarter of their budgets to in-state races. But the opposite world, the world of the PAC dwarf who exhausts its shoestring budget on an anemic list of local recipients, is more heavily populated than we had thought. These hinterland homebodies, roughly one corporate PAC in four, are among the most interesting characters we have encountered.

What is more, it appears that most corporate PACs are vulnerable to the sorts of pressures that are felt by parochial PACs with the greatest poignancy. The world of the home office is indeed more ideological, or at least more Republican, than the accommodationist world of Washington politics. Yet even among these nationalized organizations we found manifestations of localism. Corporate committees who enjoy a national vantage point, but who live without affiliated siblings, appear to bow to parochial points of view. If affiliates are there to satisfy local sentiments, on the other hand, Washington PACs are capable of an accommodationist generosity of truly impressive proportions.

Part of our evidence for these points was suggested by a comparison of the rather different elections of 1980 and 1984. Thus the partisan motivations of parochial PACs and the Republican tug of state-level forces are both more salient when viewed against the backdrop of the proincumbent and pro-Democratic retreat of the second election. Yet these points presume an argument we have yet to make: Election-specific partisan expectations are important shapers of contribution strategies. We turn now to a full consideration of the electoral environment.

Notes

1. Frank J. Sorauf, "Political Action Committees in American Politics: An Overview," in *What Price PACs?* (New York: Twentieth Century Fund, 1984), p. 94.

2. Arthur B. Krim, "Comments and Dissents," in *What Price PACs?*, p. 14.

3. David Adamany, "PACs and the Democratic Financing of Politics," *Arizona Law Review* 22, no. 2 (1980), p. 596.

4. Kirk F. Brown, "National Financing of Local Elections," paper prepared for delivery at the 1987 annual meeting of the American Political Science Association, Chicago, September 3–6, 1987.

5. Brown, "National Financing of Local Elections," p. 31.

6. Theodore J. Eismeier and Philip H. Pollock III, "Political Action Committees: Varieties of Organization and Strategy," in Michael J. Malbin, ed., *Money and Politics in the United States* (Chatham, NJ: Chatham House, 1984), pp. 122–41.

7. In 1980 corporate PACs contributed a total of $11.8 million, $3.4 million of which (roughly 29 percent) was spent in-state.

8. Richard F. Fenno, "If, As Ralph Nader Says, Congress is 'The Broken Branch,' How Come We Love Our Congressmen So Much?" in Norman J. Ornstein, ed., *Congress in Change* (New York: Praeger, 1975), pp. 277–87.

9. Edward Handler and John R. Mulkern, *Business in Politics: Campaign Strategies of Corporate Political Action Committees* (Lexington, MA: Lexington Books, 1982).

10. Eismeier and Pollock, "A Tale of Two Elections: PAC Money in 1980 and 1984," *Corruption and Reform* 1 (1986), pp. 189–207.

11. John R. Wright, "PACs, Contributions, and Roll Calls: An Organizational Perspective," *American Political Science Review* 79, no. 2 (June 1985), pp. 400–14.

12. Information on the corporate PACs in Table 4.9 was compiled from Edward Zuckerman, *Almanac of Federal PACs, 1986* (Washington, DC: Amward Publications, 1986). This resource, which provides data for political action committees that have contributed $50 thousand or more to congressional candidates, contains useful information that cannot be directly obtained from the Federal Election Commission data tapes, such as the names of all affiliated PACs and the economic sector, assets, and revenues of each PAC's corporate sponsor.

13. See, for example, Eismeier and Pollock, "An Organizational Analysis of Political Action Committees," *Political Behavior* 7, no. 2 (1985), pp. 192–216. See also Frank J. Sorauf, "Who's in Charge? Accountability in Political Action Committees," *Political Science Quarterly* 99, no. 4 (Winter 1984–1985), pp. 591–614.

5

PACs and the Campaign Environment

Thus far our treatment of the political strategies of business has emphasized those factors that affect individual organizations independently of other groups and quite apart from the larger electoral setting. In reality, of course, group behavior is not so insular. Although PACs are diverse in their motives and tactics, they operate in a relatively small world in which information shared among interest groups, political parties, candidates, and PACs may also shape decisions about in whom and how much to invest.

The possibility of collusion concerns some observers of the election economy. In Thomas B. Edsall's view, for example, it is the "coordination" among corporate PACs that gives clout to their individually modest contributions:

> Without cooperative efforts, then, individual corporate PACs would remain minor-league figures, without significant impact on the content of legislation. Cooperative action among corporate PACs has emerged through two interrelated strategies: the channeling of money to incumbent Democrats, whose votes provide the margin of victory or defeat on major issues, particularly in the House, where the Democratic majority remains firm; and the channeling of money to Republicans who are both incumbents and challengers but whose votes and overall philosophy are far more reliably favorable to business than the votes and philosophy of their Democrat counterparts.[1]

This pattern of contributions to Democratic incumbents and Republicans of all sorts, we have seen, is the product of many thousands of spending choices that differ significantly from industry to industry and from PAC to PAC. No matter what its political significance, the aggregate distribution of PAC money implies nothing about the behavior of individual PACs or collusion among them, except by the fallacy of division.

In fact, coordination is probably too blunt a term to describe adequately the complex ways in which the actions of one corporate PAC may be related to those of others. There are four conceptually distinct ways in which the aggregate spending of these PACs may be patterned. First, judgments about the electoral environment, whether arrived at independently or in consultation with others, may give a common tilt to the tactics of PACs in any given election. Second, whether or not corporate PACs seek to cooperate, their decision making is commonly affected by the dynamics of what Thomas Schelling terms contingent behavior, behavior that depends on what others are doing.[2] Third, decisions about campaign contributions may be influenced by networks of information sharing and cue giving. Finally, PACs' choices may be affected by the tugs and pulls of individual candidates and their national parties. Let us consider these each in turn.

PACs as well as potential candidates would be foolish not to keep their fingers to the winds. That these prominent players adjust their strategies according to their best readings of current political conditions is the starting point of recent theorizing about the dynamics of congressional elections.[3] Potential challengers, the argument goes, make their decisions about whether or not to run a year or so in advance of the general election, and their decisions are powerfully influenced by current economic and political conditions. When auguries are good for their party, strong candidates will be drawn into races as challengers. On the other hand, when economic woes or an unpopular president bodes ill for their party, strong candidates are likely to decide that the better part of valor is discretion and leave the field of challengers to novices. Such election-specific considerations affect the quality of the pool of candidates, notably the pool of Republican challengers, and thus the investment decisions of corporate PACs.

In addition to their effects on the candidate pool, short-term partisan forces also affect the tactics of PACs with various motives, for "contributors of all kinds follow strategies that put money into races that are expected to be close."[4] Election-specific partisan forces, such as the state of the economy or political scandal, directly affect evaluations of closeness and thus lead to predictable tactical behavior across all kinds of corporate PACs. Accommodationists, as we have called those PACs whose primary objective is access, should tilt toward incumbents of whichever party is disadvantaged by national conditions because by so doing they are putting their money where it is most needed, and presumably most valued. For adversarial PACs, the tendency to give to challengers should be exaggerated in those elections in which conditions are unfavorable for the party of targeted incumbents, who are usually Democrats. Depending on national conditions, Republican partisans among the ranks of corporate PACs may either spend heavily to shore up vulnerable Republican incumbents or venture more money to challengers to enlarge the Republican side in Congress. The net effect of these different sorts of calculations would seem to be that in auspicious years for Republicans the money of corporate PACs flows more heavily to Republican challengers but also to Democratic incumbents, and in lean years money shifts to Republican incumbents.

If choices between Republicans and Democrats as well as incumbents and challengers are influenced by the assessments made by individual PACs about national political conditions, such decisions also reflect their perceptions about what other PACs are likely to do in the campaign. Regardless of its objectives, no PAC is likely to pursue its goals by standing alone in support of hopeless candidates. This is hardly a risk with most incumbents, with whom the problem for PACs may be that their money is not especially needed or especially valued. For challengers, on the other hand, the critical mass phenomenon is likely to be crucial.[5] Most PACs are likely to invest in challengers only if they know that other contributors have already done so or reasonably expect them to do so. Thus in the elaborate mating dance of candidates and contributors, PACs' concerns about the viability of challengers' campaigns often become self-fulfilling prophecies.

In making such judgments about candidates and campaigns, PACs may rely on various informal networks for information and cues. Most corporate PACs, of course, are far removed from the insiders' world of networking in Washington. Yet even these PACs in the political hinterland are likely to rely in some way on others for political intelligence. For some PACs this may be as simple as a phone call to a counterpart in another corporation or information and guidance from the publications and PACs of their national trade associations. Small and large PACs alike may also rely on signals from bellwether organizations in Washington, whose own modest campaign contributions do not measure their real influence. The most prominent of these is the Business Industry Political Action Committee (BIPAC), with which 61 percent of corporate PACs have an affiliation:

> BIPAC contributes directly to candidates, making gifts of about $200,000 in 1982. More important, it has held monthly briefings during election seasons since 1972 for 100–125 PAC managers, in Washington and in roadshows around the country. In election years BIPAC also operates a recorded telephone service called DIAL that plays daily updates on congressional races. A BIPAC endorsement is highly prized by candidates since it sends a signal to other PACs that the selected candidate is "right" on the issues and has a reasonable chance to win. With a field staff and an extensive nationwide organization, BIPAC is well positioned to identify close races and alert its members by means of a publication it mails every few weeks. BIPAC has enhanced its influence as an early warning signal with its willingness to get involved in party primaries and to give "seed money" to favored contenders many months before the general election campaign.[6]

Large percentages of the parents of corporate PACs are affiliated with the Chamber of Commerce and the Public Affairs Council, both of which also provide information on campaigns.[7]

These national affiliations are important, although less powerful than is often claimed. The largest of corporate PACs may have their own sources of information, and the smallest, who often give only to a few local candidates, may scarcely need advice. Moreover, the interests of firms within industries are not always identical, and the issues that concern them may be different from those that concern the national trade association of the industry. This may explain why a survey of *Fortune* 500 corporations found that PACs' managers rarely mentioned trade associations as having influence on the selection of candidates.[8] Still, networks of information may be catalysts that speed up or impede the flow of funds to a candidate.

The most powerful pulls on PACs, however, are likely to come not from other suppliers of political money but rather from the demand side. Unlike challengers, who are most in need of money and least likely to receive it, incumbents can generally raise as much money from PACs and other sources as they think they require. And although there is considerable evidence that additional campaign spending has little payoff for incumbents, congressional officeholders have apparently considered it prudent to raise more and more funds at earlier and earlier times in the election cycle, if for no other reason than to scare off potential challengers.[9] Indeed, in recent elections a growing number of Democratic incumbents have tailored their images and successfully marketed themselves to corporate PACs as "business Democrats." Those incumbents in positions of power relevant to a firm's interests are, of course, especially powerful claimants on corporate PACs.

The national party organizations also seek to channel the flow of funds from PACs. As with other aspects of campaign technology and fund raising, the Republican National Committee was the first to attempt to fully exploit the resources of the growing number of political action committees, especially corporate PACs. The RNC has devoted great time and effort to cultivate these contributors, providing information about "opportunity races" in which money would presumably be well spent and identifying those PACs that are most likely to supply the venture capital crucial to challengers. Belatedly the Democratic National Committee has made a similar effort to influence political action committees, and the coordination of PAC spending, some now argue, has contributed to the recent strengthening of the national parties.[10]

The judgments of PACs about the circumstances of specific elections as well as the evolving relationships among PACs and between PACs and other actors have produced important aggregate shifts in the contributions of corporate PACs in the last decade, which are reported in Table 5.1. The election of 1978, when the Federal Election Commission first began reporting such detailed information on PAC contributions, also marked an important turning point in the strategies of many corporate PACs. For much of the 1970s the aggregate

Table 5.1
Proportions of Contributions of Corporate PACs to
Six Types of House and Senate Candidates, 1978-1986

	House				
	1978	1980	1982	1984	1986
Democratic Incumbents	35%	36%	32%	43%	43%
Democratic Challengers	2	1	1	1	1
Democratic Open Seats	7	1	3	1	3
Republican Incumbents	28	32	45	39	41
Republican Challengers	16	20	9	10	3
Republican Open Seats	12	9	9	7	9
Totals	100%	99%	99%	101%	100%

	Senate				
	1978	1980	1982	1984	1986
Democratic Incumbents	15%	25%	26%	20%	13%
Democratic Challengers	6	1	1	2	7
Democratic Open Seats	7	2	1	4	4
Republican Incumbents	37	14	41	58	48
Republican Challengers	20	47	17	6	7
Republican Open Seats	15	11	14	11	21
Totals	100%	100%	100%	101%	100%

contributions of corporate committee were very evenly divided between Democrats and Republicans and went overwhelmingly to incumbents. Indeed, in 1978 Ronald Reagan chided a business audience for their timidity: "I don't think the Republican Party has received the kind of support from corporate PACs that its record deserves. Why does half of the business PAC money go to candidates who may not be friends of business? The best thing you can hope for by following an anti-business incumbent contribution strategy is that the alligator will eat you last."[11] The Republican tilt of corporate PACs in that year presaged their unprecedented partisanship and risk taking in the 1980 election. Yet although Republican partisanship has reappeared in this decade, corporate PACs have been loath to spend as heavily on House or Senate challengers. A closer look at the elections of the 1980s will show how the place of corporate PACs in the larger political environment has changed and provide some clues about its future.

1980: The Triumph of Partisanship

By all accounts the 1980 election was a partisan cataclysm. Not only was an incumbent president turned out of office in a landslide but Republicans captured thirty-three new House seats and a Senate majority for the first time in a generation. Among the several proximate causes of the upheaval in congressional elections was the unprecedented pouring of PAC money, especially that of corporate PACs, into the campaigns of Republican challengers and candidates for open seats. The spending of corporate PACs in both House and Senate elections nearly doubled between 1978 and 1980, and a large share of this increase went to Republican nonincumbents. The $3.4 million spent by corporate PACs on Republican challengers and open-seat candidates for the House was nearly as much as was spent on either Republican or Democratic incumbents. In Senate races these PACs spent almost half of their budgets, $3.2 million, on Republican challengers, and much of this went to races in smaller states, where its impact was significant.[12]

The timing of these contributions also worked to the advantage of Republicans. Early money is especially important for challengers, who must demonstrate the viability of their campaigns in order to attract the large sums of money needed to wage an effective race. Political action committees, many of which are not prone to great risks, have never been an easily cultivated source of this seed money. In 1980, however, corporate PACs began to fund Republican challengers sooner than they had in previous elections. And when the potential magnitude of the Republican victory became clear in the waning days of the campaign, money was thrown into these campaigns. In some races these last-minute contributions from PACs were decisive. As Representative Leon Panetta described it, "labor couldn't expand its ability to raise money, while business was mushrooming. In the 1980 election we could see that a Republican challenger had the ability to get two or three hundred thousand dollars in the last weeks of a campaign and knock off the incumbent."[13]

The pronounced shift toward Republican challengers was the product of the coincidence of several factors, all of which inclined corporate PACs toward adversarialism. To begin with, the shift reflected a profound antipathy on the part of many corporations to the Carter administration and the Democratic Congress, an antipathy engendered both by the performance of the economy as well as by the grievances of various industries over policy. The oil and gas industry, we have seen, spent heavily against Democratic incumbents after what it perceived to be a betrayal over natural gas deregulation. And these PACs were joined by those of the chemical industry in supporting the opponents of congressional supporters of "superfund" legislation.[14] Even some of those in the business community who had served as major fund-raisers for the Democrats—including Steven Ross, the chairman of Warner Communications—had by 1980 been put off by differences with the Carter White House.[15]

Of course, even in the absence of a bill of particulars against the party in power, PACs otherwise inclined to help expand the Republican cohort in Congress were presented with an unusual opportunity in 1980. On the Senate side the twenty-four Democratic seats that had last been won in the aftermath of Watergate, and several incumbents—Birch Bayh of Indiana, Frank Church of Idaho, John Culver of Iowa, George McGovern of South Dakota to name a few—were in vulnerable positions. On the House side the Democrats' looming difficulties had attracted to the field a set of strong Republican challengers whose campaigns were buoyed by a wave of discontent against Democrats that PACs had sensed as the election approached.

Information about candidates and campaigns, which helped attract money to these challengers, was made all the more important by the elaborate networks among Corporate PACs that had developed. By the 1980 election BIPAC and others were supplying large numbers of PACs with information about electoral conditions as well as particular races. When these bellwethers began suggesting that a Republican sweep was possible and perhaps likely, what might have been a trickle of contributions to challengers quickly became a flood.

By 1980, moreover, the Republican party had in place a sophisticated mechanism for identifying potential donors, supplying information of its own about races, and using its persuasive powers to influence PACs' decisions. "The PACs are supporting challengers more," concluded then RNC Chairman William Brock. "We really worked on that in 1980. We said 'the business of business is to take risks.' We managed to get PACs to give a third of their money to challengers."[16] The Democratic party, which lagged behind the Republican party in recognizing the importance of PACs and developing adaptive strategies, was caught flatfooted. Although Democratic incumbents in the House and Senate still managed to raise as much, on average, as Republicans, Republican challengers and open-seat candidates raised substantially more from PACs than Democrats. Corporate PACs made the difference.

For Democrats the 1980 election was a cloud with a dark lining. Not only were the White House and Senate lost and the House majority diminished, but this was made possible in part by the powerful allies the Republicans had found among corporate PACs. The election demonstrated that under the right circumstances—poignant grievances over policy, omens of electoral change, information networks magnifying bandwagon effects, and a mismatch in the efforts of parties to cultivate PACs—corporate PACs could be transformed into Republican shock troops. Whether this transformation would become permanent became one of the open questions of the new American politics.

1982: Circling the Wagons Around Republicans

The midterm elections of 1982 were an important test of the durability of the incipient party realignment that some Republicans saw in the Reagan landslide and the stunning legislative victories of 1981. Indeed, the bright prospects of 1981 had lured to the field another set of strong Republican challengers in the House, and the Senate Democrats were defending eight more seats than Republicans. Republican strategists thus had reason to hope that their Senate majority might be increased and that the losses in the House attendant to the president's party in midterm elections could be minimized. In the view of Republican optimists there was even a possibility that 1982 would be the first midterm election since 1932 in which the president's party gained, not lost seats.

As the election approached, however, Republican prospects dimmed considerably. To begin with, the promise of supply-side economics had been followed by a deep recession in 1982, which produced unemployment rates of more than 9 percent. "Stay the course" slogans notwithstanding, the recession had hurt the president's popularity and even sowed the seeds of dissent within the ranks of congressional Republicans. There was good reason to be skittish. Nineteen of the freshmen Republicans in the House had won election by 2 percent of the vote or less, and the Democrats had begun to wage an effective campaign on the issues of the economy, fairness, and a nuclear freeze. These developments all but dashed Republican hopes for evidence of a realignment in 1982 and even put in jeopardy the gains of 1980.[17]

Recognizing these risks, the Republican National Committee made an extraordinary effort to mobilize the resources of PACs. "The big story of the campaign," observed Deputy Assistant to the President for Political Affairs Lee Atwater, "is that this is the first time the White House has really been involved with the political action committees since their birth. Carter didn't really do anything with them. We have a full time PAC operation at the Republican National Committee, under Rick Shelby."[18] As the effort was described by Atwater, "the congressional campaign committee and the Republican National Committee are having meetings with every PAC in town and saying, 'Here's the targeted list sanctioned by the RNC, the congressional committee, and the White House.' "[19]

Stung by the Republican partisanship of corporate PACs in 1980, Democrats in the House and Senate mounted their own campaigns to attract business money. The effort of Democrats to outbid the Republicans in the cutting of taxes for business in 1981, some have suggested, was mainly an effort to recoup the losses of the year before. This certainly appeared to be the case for the provisions affecting the oil industry. "I felt it was not only good energy policy," Representative Richard Gephardt argued, "but also would allow us to show domestic drillers that we were not down on everything they were for—which was their impression. If you look at the 1980 campaign, you'll find incredible amounts of oil money going into Republican campaigns."[20] Beyond these collective efforts to regain the support of business, a growing number of Democratic incumbents had begun to tailor their images in order to market themselves to corporate PACs as "business Democrats."[21]

The very different circumstances of the 1982 election produced a remarkable change in the spending of corporate PACs. In all, the proportion of spending on Republican challengers fell from 20 percent to 9 percent in the House and from 47 percent to 17 percent in Senate races; spending on Republican incumbents

Table 5.2
Corporate PAC Tactical Shifts: 1980 and 1982 House Elections

Largest Percent of 1982 Contributions Allocated to:	Largest Percent of 1980 Contributions Allocated to:			
	Republican Incumbents	Republican Challengers	Democratic Incumbents	1982 Totals
Republican Incumbents	87% (286)	69% (119)	34% (155)	59% (560)
Republican Challengers	4 (12)	16 (27)	3 (15)	6% (54)
Democratic Incumbents	8 (27)	14 (24)	62 (280)	35% (331)
1980 Totals	34% (325)	18% (170)	47% (450)	100% (945)

increased from 32 percent to 44 percent in the House and from 14 percent to 41 percent in the Senate.[22] These aggregate changes reflect a good deal of tactical switching by individual PACs, which is reported in Table 5.2. The table shows the extent to which corporate PACs favoring one type of House candidate in 1980—that is to say, allocating the largest share of their budgets to that type— changed their allocation to favor another type of candidate in 1982.[23] The least amount of switching of preferences is found among the third of corporate PACs that spent the largest share of their budgets on Republican incumbents; in 1982, 87 percent of these continued to do so. The largest group of PACs in 1980 were the 47 percent that allocated the greatest proportions of their budgets to Democratic incumbents. Among these accommodationists there was considerably more shifting between elections, as more than a third spent the largest share of their budgets on Republican incumbents in 1982. The greatest tactical shift, however, came from the PACs that had devoted the best part of their spending to Republican challengers in 1980. In 1982 more than two-thirds of these PACs had adjusted their spending so that the largest share went instead to Republican incumbents.

Although PACs of all sorts were more attracted to Republicans in 1982, not all targeted their funds in the same way. Table 5.3 groups the PACs according to their tactical shifts between 1980 and 1982:

Stalwart Republicans gave the largest share of their money to Republican incumbents in 1980 and 1982.

Strategic Republicans gave the largest share of their money to Republican challengers in 1980 and Republican incumbents in 1982.

Republican venture capitalists gave the largest share of their money to Republican challengers in 1980 and 1982.

Table 5.3
Targeting of Spending to Marginal Races by
Various Types of Corporate PACs, 1982 House Elections

PAC Type:	Percent of Contributions to Each Candidate Type Targeted to Marginal Races:		
	Republican Incumbents	Democratic Incumbents	Republican Challengers
Stalwart Republicans (N=286)	46%	27%	64%
Strategic Republicans (N=119)	62%	24%	66%
Republican Venture Capitalists (N=27)	61%	18%	68%
Pragmatists (N=155)	44%	27%	63%
Democratic Accommodationists (N=280)	37%	27%	63%

Pragmatists gave the largest share of their money to Democratic incumbents in 1980 and Republican incumbents in 1982.

Democratic accommodationists gave the largest share of their money to Democratic incumbents in 1980 and 1982.

Table 5.3 then shows for each grouping the average proportion of spending on Republican incumbents, Democratic incumbents, and Republican challengers in 1982 that went to marginal races—those races where the winning candidate in 1980 received less than 60 percent of the vote.

Several conclusions from Table 5.3 bear emphasis. It comes as no surprise that of the money they spent on challengers, PACs of all tactical types targeted most of it for marginal races. More surprising perhaps is how little of the money spent by the typical PAC on Democratic incumbents was targeted to marginals, ranging across the groups from less than one dollar in five to only slightly more than one dollar in four. Democratic accommodationists were not much more efficient in their targeting of funds in races involving Republican incumbents; only 37 percent of their spending on these candidates went to marginals. Interestingly, the most efficient targeting was done by those corporate PACs that in 1980 had favored Republican challengers. Apparently wanting to keep in office the insurgents they had helped in 1980, these PACs devoted more than 60 percent of the money they spent on Republican incumbents to those who were most vulnerable.

Indeed, by some accounts it was the lavish funding of Republican marginals by PACs and others that helped to keep the Republican majority in the Senate and to limit Republican losses in the House to twenty-six seats, a good deal less than expected in a midterm election during a recession.[24] Corporate PACs, many of which had joined the Republican offensive in 1980 by supporting challengers, showed flexibility and savvy by spending defensively but efficiently in 1982. To be sure, the effort of Democratic incumbents to woo business PACs, and thereby keep money away from challengers, had paid dividends. Yet in the first two elections of the 1980s an important partisan asymmetry was developing. PAC money for Republicans was highly mobile, shifting from challengers in auspicious years to incumbents in lean years. In contrast, PAC money for Democrats—including that of labor PACs—was much stickier. Even under the most favorable of conditions Democratic challengers were relatively starved of PAC contributions, starved in no small measure by the insatiable appetites for money of safe but nervous Democratic incumbents. It was this asymmetry, not the relatively equal amounts of money that the two parties raised from all PACs, that constituted an important part of the growing Republican advantage in campaign finance.[25]

1984: The Retreat from Partisanship

With the benefit of hindsight the 1984 election appears to have been a great opportunity for Republicans to exploit their fluid PAC resources in the same way they had done in 1980. Gary Hart's campaign barb that nominating Walter Mondale would mean a rerun of the Democratic disaster of 1980 proved to be an understatement. Mondale won only his own state of Minnesota, and the slim majority won by Ronald Reagan in the three-way race of 1980 increased to nearly 60 percent of the popular vote in 1984. Moreover, there were signs of significant change in the electorate's views of the parties and in their attachments to them, signs that led some observers to suggest that a realignment of the parties was under way.[26] All of this, one might have thought, would have produced the same kind of impressive investments in Republican challengers that had been made in 1980.

It did not. Tables 5.4 and 5.5, which report the quarterly contributions per candidate by corporate PACs to Democratic incumbents, Republican incumbents, and Republican challengers in the 1979–1980 and 1983–1984 election cycles, show striking differences in patterns of spending. In the 1980 Senate races, early contributions to incumbents of both parties were matched by a late surge of spending on Republican challengers so that, on average, these candidates received substantially more from corporate PACs than Democratic incumbents and as much as Republican incumbents. In 1984 the only surge of money from corporate PACs went to Republican incumbents. On average, Republicans challenging for Senate seats received only $13,200 from corporate PACs, less than 10 percent of what challengers had gotten in 1980. Mitch

Table 5.4
**Quarterly Spending of Corporate PACs in Senate Races:
1979–1980 and 1983–1984 Election Cycles**

| Year and Quarter: | Per Candidate Contributions, in Thousands: | | | | | |
| | Democratic Incumbents | | Republican Incumbents | | Republican Challengers | |
	1980	1984	1980	1984	1980	1984
Year before election						
Winter	1.9	21.5	2.4	19.0	0	0
Spring	8.1	34.5	7.0	38.0	1.8	.1
Summer	7.6	12.8	2.8	19.1	.9	0
Fall	10.8	14.2	6.4	21.3	2.0	.1
Election year						
Winter	15.8	23.5	11.6	54.8	8.0	.2
Spring	23.6	35.4	29.2	82.3	30.6	1.8
Summer	32.1	34.1	44.4	98.2	72.2	1.7
Fall	16.3	23.7	38.4	69.0	28.3	9.5
Totals	$116.2	$199.7	$142.2	$401.7	$143.8	$13.2
Ratio to spending for Republican incumbents	.82	.50	1.00	1.00	1.01	.03

McConnell was the only Republican challenger to win, while Democrats picked up one open seat and defeated incumbents Roger Jepsen and Charles Percy for a net gain of two.

Senate elections, of course, are idiosyncratic, and in 1984 the Republicans defended several vulnerable seats and faced a formidable set of Democratic incumbents.[27] However, Table 5.5 documents a similar if more muted retreat in House elections. Again, the surge of money from corporate PACs to Republican challengers that took place in 1980 never occurred in 1984. In 1980 Republican challengers received, on average, more than $23,000 from corporate PACs as compared to $20,000 for Democratic incumbents and $38,000 for Republican incumbents. In 1984 the contributions of corporate PACs grew to an average of $40,000 for Democratic incumbents and $62,000 for Republican incumbents while contributions to Republican challengers fell to an average of only $8,000. Democratic incumbents were very active in raising money from corporate PACs and others in 1983, and perhaps partly as a result only thirteen were defeated. Including open-seat races, the net gain for the Republicans in the House was only fourteen, a far cry from the swing of thirty-four seats in 1980.

Certainly there are a number of differences between the elections of 1980 and 1984 that help to explain the apparent timidity of corporate PACs.[28] Clearly the Senate offered fewer opportunities for the Republicans. In the House uncertain-

Table 5.5
Quarterly Spending of Corporate PACs in House Races:
1979-1980 and 1983-1984 Election Cycles

Year and Quarter:	Per Candidate Contributions, in Thousands:					
	Democratic Incumbents		Republican Incumbents		Republican Challengers**	
	1980	1984	1980	1984	1980	1984
Year before election						
Winter	.1	1.0	1.3	.8	*	*
Spring	.7	3.1	.7	3.8	*	*
Summer	.9	3.3	2.7	3.3	*	*
Fall	1.3	3.8	2.8	4.4	.1	*
Election year						
Winter	2.4	3.9	4.9	5.8	1.0	.1
Spring	4.2	7.7	6.9	13.3	3.7	1.1
Summer	6.0	9.6	11.4	17.7	9.5	2.7
Fall	4.4	7.7	7.3	13.1	8.8	4.4
Totals	$20.0	$40.1	$38.0	$62.2	$23.1	$8.3
Ratio to spending for Republican incumbents	.53	.64	1.00	1.00	.61	.13

* Less than $100.

** Excludes token candidates, defined as those challengers who won
   less than 20 percent of the vote in the general election.

ties about the election and Reagan's popularity as well as the disappointing showing of Republican challengers in 1982 apparently produced a weaker crop of Republican challengers than the two previous elections. Moreover, not only had the ranks of vulnerable Democratic incumbents been depleted in 1980, but those who remained were running hard. The best opportunities for partisan take-overs are in open-seat races, but in 1984 there were only thirteen such seats that had been held by Democrats as compared to twenty-seven in 1980. All of this may have suggested a course of prudence to corporate PACs.

Yet there are reasons beyond these election-specific considerations for the defensiveness of corporate PACs in 1984. One important reason was the effective counteroffensive launched by the Democrats in 1984. Chastened by the 1980 debacle—"What had happened, in 1980, we had our asses kicked," said Chairman of the Democratic Congressional Campaign Committee Tony Coelho[29]—Democrats developed a carrot-and-stick strategy for dealing with business interests. On the one hand, many incumbent Democrats continued to build pro-business images and to trade on the power of incumbency. On the other hand, even as business PACs were reminded of the benefits of pragmatism they were alerted to the risks of partisanship. Representative Coelho is said to have put it this way to the corporate PACs that had become increasingly partisan in the 1980s: "You people are determined to get rid of the Democratic Party. The records show it. I just want you to know we are going to be in the majority of the House for many, many years and I don't think it makes good business sense for you to try to destroy us."[30] Faced with such an ultimatum, many corporate PACs apparently decided that the better part of valor was discretion.

In some respects the Republicans were also victims of their own success, for in defeating the Carter administration they had lost the perfect foil for their appeals for business support. Moreover, with the help of the Republican-controlled Senate the Reagan administration had already gone some distance in enacting and implementing the probusiness platform on which it had run unabashedly in 1980. From cuts in taxes to regulatory relief to flexibility in antitrust policy, the Reagan administration had in fact served what business perceived to be its collective interest. Yet gratitude is fleeting in politics. For many corporations there were still a host of specific issues on which incumbents of both parties could be of service. And many corporate PACs decided to rest content with the partial realignment of party and policy that had occurred in 1980 and return to business as usual in pursuing narrower interests.

1986: The Battle for the Senate

The Republicans' failure in 1984 to solidify their hold on the Senate would put this important vantage point in great jeopardy in 1986, when circumstances would favor the Democrats. To begin with, twenty-two Republican seats were up for reelection as opposed to only twelve Democratic seats. Moreover, this was the first electoral test for the Republican class of 1980, many of whom had won by razor-thin margins with Ronald Reagan at the top of the ticket. Many of this class—James Abnor of South Dakota, Mark Andrews of North Dakota, Jeremiah Denton of Alabama, Slade Gorton of Washington State, Paula Hawkins of Florida, Robert Kasten of Wisconsin, Mack Mattingly of Georgia, Steven Symms of Idaho—were clearly vulnerable as they now had to run on their own against formidable Democratic challengers.

Republican prospects in the House were considerably brighter. Their small numbers alone made it unlikely that the Republicans would suffer the large losses typical for a president's second midterm during the twentieth century, and the party was also helped by their president's unprecedented popularity as well as the general health of the American economy. The forty-four open seats would be an important battleground in House elections, as would be many districts in the South, which were now among the nation's most competitive.

The real battle of 1986, however, was for the Senate, and the resources of corporate PACs shifted dramatically to those races. In the first three elections of the 1980s corporate PACs had spent two dollars in House races for every one dollar in Senate races; in 1986, 44 percent of their contributions went to the

Senate. In all, corporate PACs spent $19 million on Senate candidates running in 1986, as compared to only $11 million in 1984. About half of this money went to Republican incumbents, who raised on average from corporate PACs $550,000 each and twice as much as Democratic incumbents. The Republican candidates for open seats received even more, an average of $650,000 each. Spending on Republican challengers for the Senate was heavily concentrated on those few—California's Ed Zschau received by far the most—who were attractive to business and stood a chance of winning.

In the House the contributions to corporate PACs grew only to $27 million from the $23 million that had been spent in 1984, and the distribution of this money reflected the same tilt toward incumbents as the previous two elections. Between 1984 and 1986 the average contribution of corporate PACs to Republican incumbents rose from $62,000 to $72,000 and that of Democratic incumbents from $40,000 to $50,000. The Democrats' success in putting the genie of corporate PACs back in the bottle was evident in the lack of support for Republican challengers, who averaged only $5,000 each in contributions from these committees. Not only did the efforts of the Democratic campaign committee to court business continue to pay dividends, but firms from the oil and gas industry, which had been the largest single source of Republican venture capital, had fallen on hard times.[31] Still the most powerful force in House elections continued to be that of incumbents, a record proportion of whom were re-elected. As they had done with other parts of their electoral environment during the 1970s, incumbents had during the 1980s gone a long way toward managing the potential threat posed by PACs.

In the Senate, however, incumbency made much less of a difference. In elections as close as those of 1980, seven Republican incumbents were defeated as the Democrats gained eight seats and control of the Senate. The campaign funding of these incumbents, along with the president's personal campaigning, probably made these races as close as they were. Yet for the first time in this decade a substantial number of Democratic challengers were able to amass enough resources from a variety of sources—including labor PACs and the growing number of liberal nonconnected PACs—to mount effective campaigns and exploit weak opponents as well as local issues.

The result was a far cry from the 1980 election, when corporate PACs had spent some $18 million and were widely credited with helping to effect a major change in politics and policy. In 1986 corporate PACs spent $46 million with little to show for it save perhaps the fleeting gratitude of incumbents of both parties, whose demands for funds were apparently insatiable. It is little wonder that in the wake of the election many business PACs were left wondering about the efficacy of their activities. Partisans among the ranks of corporate PACs were no doubt disappointed by the failure of the Republicans to hold the Senate. Yet pragmatists could also find little solace in this election. Ironically, the flood of money into congressional elections appeared to have created a lobbying gridlock, an environment of such diverse and conflicting monied interests that on important matters such as tax reform members of Congress were able to ignore most of them.[32]

1988 and Beyond

The elections of the 1980s have demonstrated both the potential volatility of the American electoral system and the powerful forces keeping the system at an equilibrium. The decade began with two presidential landslides for the Republicans and indications of major gains in the party's strength in the electorate. However, aside from the temporary loss of the Senate, the Democrats' hold on seats in Congress has remained remarkably strong, and the Democrats have regained much of the advantage in party identification they once held over the Republicans. The maturing of corporate PACs during this period was very much a part of these developments. The elections of 1980 and 1982 demonstrated that under the right circumstances the growing networks of business PACs could be a powerful partisan force. The elections of 1984 and 1986, on the other hand, demonstrated the ability of Democrats to cope with the PAC shock by their own appeals to the diverse and pragmatic interests of business and by the mining of additional sources of money.

Yet the current equilibrium in the economy of congressional elections is by no means a stable one. The future role of corporate PACs will be affected not only by their own organizational evolution but also by changes in the laws regulating their behavior and by the changing environment of politics and policy in which they operate. What the future holds for these important new players in American politics is the subject of the concluding chapter.

Notes

1. Thomas B. Edsall, *The New Politics of Inequality* (New York: W. W. Norton and Co., 1984), pp. 132–33. See also Dan Clawson, Alan Neustadl, and James Bearden, "The Logic of Business Unity: Corporate Contributions in the 1980 Congressional Elections," *American Sociological Review* 51, no. 6 (December 1986), pp. 797–811.

2. Thomas Schelling, *Micromotives and Macrobehavior* (New York: W. W. Norton and Co., 1978), p. 17.

3. Gary C. Jacobson and Samuel J. Kernell, *Strategy and Choice in Congressional Elections* (New Haven, CT: Yale University Press, 1981). See also Theodore J. Eismeier and Philip H. Pollock III, "Strategy and Choice in Congressional Elections: The Role of Political Action Committees," *American Journal of Political Science* 30, no. 1 (February 1986), pp. 197–213.

4. Jacobsen and Kernell, *Strategy and Choice in Congressional Elections*, p. 39.

5. Critical mass phenomena are discussed in Schelling, *Micromotives and Macrobehavior*, ch. 3.

6. Larry J. Sabato, *PAC Power* (New York: W. W. Norton and Co., 1985), p. 47.

7. Ibid., p. 45.

8. Anne B. Matasar, *Corporate PACs and the Federal Campaign Financing Laws* (Westport, CT: Quorum Books, 1986), pp. 73–74.

9. Gary C. Jacobson, *The Politics of Congressional Elections* (Boston: Little, Brown, 1987); Edie N. Goldenberg and Michael W. Traugott, *Campaigning for Congress* (Washington, DC: Congressional Quarterly Press, 1984).

10. David Adamany, "Political Parties in the 1980's," in Michael J. Malbin, ed., *Money and Politics in the United States* (Chatham, NJ: Chatham House, 1984), pp. 70–121; A. James Reichley, "The Rise of National Parties," in John E. Chubb and Paul E. Peterson, eds., *The New Direction in American Politics* (Washington, DC: The Brookings Institution, 1985), pp. 175–202.

11. Maxwell Glen, "At the Wire, Corporate PACs Come Through for the GOP," *National Journal* (February 3, 1979), p. 174.

12. Kirk F. Brown, "National Financing of Local Elections," paper delivered at the annual meeting of the American Political Science Association, Chicago, September 3–6, 1987.

13. Elizabeth Drew, *Politics and Money* (New York: Macmillan, 1983), p. 21.

14. Ibid., p. 21.

15. Ibid., p. 47. See also Thomas Ferguson and Joel Rogers, "The Reagan Victory: Corporate Coalitions in the 1980 Campaign," in Thomas Ferguson and Joel Rogers, eds., *The Hidden Election* (New York: Pantheon Books, 1981), pp. 3–64.

16. Drew, *Politics and Money*, p. 21.

17. Albert R. Hunt, "National Politics and the 1982 Campaign," in Thomas E. Mann and Norman J. Ornstein, eds., *The American Elections of 1982* (Washington, DC: American Enterprise Institute, 1983), pp. 1–43.

18. Drew, *Politics and Money*, p. 24.

19. Ibid., p. 25.

20. Ibid., p. 50.

21. For a case study, see Dennis Farney, "A Liberal Congressman Turns Conservative: Did PACs Do It?" *Wall Street Journal* (July 29, 1982), p. 1.

22. Of course, part of this change is accounted for by the fact that there were more Republican incumbents running in 1982. Yet even when the number of candidates is controlled for by dividing the percentage of total corporate PAC spending to each type of candidate by the percentage of all candidates that type comprises, differences between the 1980 and 1982 elections are apparent. For the House the ratios are 1.84 in 1980 and 2.20 in 1982; Republican open-seat candidates, 1.70 and 1.29; Republican challengers, .78 and .43; Democratic incumbents, 1.17 and 1.25; Democratic open-seat candidates, .57 and .43; Democratic challengers, .06 and .05. For the Senate the ratios are: Republican incumbents, 1.36 in 1980 and 2.46 in 1982; Republican open-seat candidates, .75 and 3.04; Republican challengers, 1.88 and .59; Democratic incumbents, 1.00 and .91; Democratic open-seat candidates, .14 and .22; Democratic challengers, .10 and .06.

23. The fifty-five PACs that allocated equal proportions of their budgets to two or more types of candidates are not included in this analysis. Spending on open-seat candidates is not considered here.

24. Gary C. Jacobson, "Money in the 1980 and 1982 Congressional Elections," in Michael J. Malbin, ed., *Money and Politics in the United States* (Chatham, NJ: Chatham House, 1984), pp. 38–69.

25. Eismeier and Pollock, "Strategy and Choice in Congressional Elections: The Role of Political Action Committees"; Gary C. Jacobson, "The Republican Advantage in Campaign Finance," in John E. Chubb and Paul E. Peterson, eds., *The New Direction in American Politics* (Washington, DC: The Brookings Institution, 1985), pp. 143–74.

26. See for example Thomas E. Cavanagh and James L. Sundquist, "The New Two Party System," in John E. Chubb and Paul E. Peterson, eds., *The New Direction in American Politics*, pp. 35–68.

27. Republican incumbents in serious races included Charles Percy of Illinois, Roger Jepsen of Iowa, Rudy Boschwitz of Minnesota, Gordon Humphrey of New Hampshire, and Jesse Helms of North Carolina. These races along with Phil Gramm's race for the open seat in Texas attracted the lion's share of Republican PAC money in the Senate. The reelected Democrats included Howell Heflin of Alabama, David Pryor of Arkansas, Joseph Biden of Delaware, Sam Nunn of Georgia, Bennett Johnston of Louisiana, Carl Levin of Michigan, Max Baucus of Montana, James Exon of Nebraska, Bill Bradley of New Jersey, David Boren of Oklahoma, and Claiborne Pell of Rhode Island.

28. We draw here on Gary C. Jacobson, "Congress: Politics After a Landslide Without Coattails," in Michael Nelson, ed., *The Elections of 1984* (Washington, DC: Congressional Quarterly Press, 1985), pp. 215–38.

29. Thomas B. Edsall, "If You've Got the Dime, Coelho's Got the Ear," *Washington Post National Weekly Edition* (December 23, 1985), p. 14.

30. Ibid., p. 14.

31. Tom Watson, "Oil's Campaign Capital Running Dry," *CQ Weekly Reports* (May 17, 1986), pp. 1109–12.

32. Burt Solomon, "When Fat Cats Cry Foul: Last Fall's Record Round of Money-Grubbing Left Business Lobbyists Annoyed with the Fund-Raising System and Unsure They Are Getting Their Money's Worth." *National Journal* 19 (February 21, 1987), pp. 418–22.

6

Looking Ahead

Caution is the watchword in any effort to foretell the future of American campaign finances, let alone the role of business in politics. After all, the thousands of extant political action committees, which now account for a quarter of contributions to Senate campaigns and a third of contributions to House races, were scarcely anticipated when Congress enacted the Federal Election Campaign Act amendments little more than a decade ago. The past and future of PACs, moreover, cannot be understood apart from the broader context of change in American politics. "The significance of the PAC," Frank J. Sorauf has observed, "is clearly more important as symptom than cause. It is at bottom a reflection of and an addition to a more fragmented American politics. It is in many ways the quintessential political organization of a time in which refinement and nuance of political expression have, at least for the moment, become more important than the capacity to govern."[1] By its very nature a fragmented politics tends to be highly volatile, so that the decade ahead may bring with it changes in campaign finances as far reaching as those that just occurred.

The future course of corporate PACs may be the most difficult to chart. These have not only been the fastest growing species of PAC but also the most diverse and protean. Giants and dwarfs, pragmatists and partisans, locals and nationals, amateurs and professionals—these, we have seen, are all parts of the puzzle of corporate PACs, and we have also seen that corporate PACs have been peculiarly affected by the shifting tides of politics and policy in the United States. Yet we have come some distance in understanding these organizations and are now in the position at least to identify those forces that will shape the political behavior of corporations in the years ahead.

The Politics of Campaign Finance Reform

Just as it was an effort at reform that helped to create political action committees, these organizations are likely to be affected significantly by future changes
in the laws regulating political money. Since 1974 legislation to modify the
federal election laws has been considered, sometimes more seriously than others,
in almost every session of Congress. In fact, as it has been interpreted by the
courts in *Buckley v. Valeo* and other decisions, amended by Congress in 1976 and
1979, and implemented by the Federal Election Commission, the law and administration of campaign finance regulations have been altered considerably
even since the sweeping changes wrought by the FECA amendments of 1974.[2]

More fundamental changes may be afoot, for to its legion of critics the
current system of financing congressional elections badly distorts law making as
well as campaigning. To the extent that there is an orthodoxy among reformers
it is this: The public interest would be served by reducing the importance of
political action committees, perhaps by replacing all or part of their contributions with other sources of money, and by limiting the escalating costs of campaigning. The specific means to achieve these desiderata, however, have varied a
good deal in the numerous proposals for comprehensive reform introduced in
Congress in the last decade.

The strongest impulse of reform has been to legislate away the influence of
PACs by lowering limits on their contributions and placing limits on the amount
of PAC money that can be accepted by candidates. This was the centerpiece of
the Obey-Railsback bill, which passed the House in 1979 only to be killed by
filibuster in the Senate.[3] Obey-Railsback would have reduced from $10,000 to
$6,000 the amount a PAC could contribute to one candidate for primary and
general elections combined and prohibited a House candidate from accepting
more than $70,000 from all PACs during a two-year election cycle. Legislation
introduced in 1985 by Senator David Boren was in the same spirit; it would have
raised the limit on individual contributions to $1,500, lowered the limit on PAC
contributions to $3,000 per candidate per election, and limited aggregate
receipts from PACs in the general election to $100,000 for House candidates
and a range of $175,000 to $750,000 for Senate candidates.[4]

Limits on PAC contributions and receipts have also been proposed in conjunction with public financing and constraints on campaign spending. In the
House one such proposal would have provided matching grants for small individual contributions, limited a candidate's PAC receipts to $90,00, and limited
general election expenditures to $200,000 for candidates who accepted public
financing. Candidates would also have been indemnified both against opponents
who exceeded the limits and against independent spending directed against
them.[5] Recent proposals in the Senate would work in much the same way,
although in the interest of cost saving some versions would introduce public
subsidies only in those races in which a candidate's opponent had exceeded a
spending limit.

Legislation that combines limits on PAC money with limits on campaign spending and modest public subsidies is not the only variant of reform,[6] but it is by far the most popular in Congress. Its central premise—that private money makes bad public policy—is deeply rooted in the American reform tradition, and its apparent simplicity and directness are appealing. Although the actual consequences of reform are likely to be anything but simple, the best thinking on the subject raises many warnings about "reform." One suspects, for example, that any combination of money limits and public subsidies devised by incumbent members of Congress is more likely to hinder than to help challengers, who in House elections especially already face long odds of winning. Lower limits on direct contributions are likely only to worsen the problem of independent spending, which was protected from limitation by *Buckley v. Valeo* and is now largely the preserve of a few large nonconnected PACs, and the various schemes to cope with this by-product of reform are not plainly fair or workable. Of course, these might well be risks worth taking in pursuit of better systems of campaigning and representation. Yet a persuasive case has not been made that limiting spending will improve the quality of campaigning. Nor has the case been made that new restrictions on campaign money will do much to change representation and policy making in Congress. In this regard Michael J. Malbin is certainly justified in his skepticism about a

> strategy of limits that fails to recognize that the fundamental source of interest-group power has little to do with campaign finance. Interest groups are what they are in the United States because parties, governmental institutions, communications, and human nature are what they are. Any attempt to deal with what is essentially a surface symptom, the contemporary electoral role of organized groups, solely through direct regulation and limits can do little more than shift group power around and weaken electoral competition.[7]

Leaving aside questions about their desirability, what would be the effects of these changes in law on corporate PACs? On the face of it corporate PACs would seem to be less affected by limits on contributions than nonconnected PACs or those of labor unions or trade associations. For one thing, a relatively small proportion of the contributions of corporate PACs approach the existing limit or exceed any of the proposed limits. There is evidence, moreover, that for a variety of organizational and legal reasons most corporate PACs are ill disposed to engage in independent spending.[8] This is certainly the case for the hundreds of small corporate committees, whose amateur staffs have neither the time, skill, nor inclination to do more than write checks to candidates. And even the largest corporate committees, some of whose contributions might be affected by limits, are far more likely to spread contributions among more candidates— perhaps giving more to challengers and marginal races and less to the most secure wielders of power in Congress—than to spend independently.

How limits on candidates' total receipts from PACs would affect PACs and campaigns, aside from the obvious effect that PACs might have to scramble to get their contributions to popular incumbents before the limits were reached, depends on the size of the limits. On the one hand, anything that restricts the flow of funds, including restrictions on campaign spending as well as restrictions on receipts from PACs, tends to work to the disadvantage of challengers. For example, by one estimate fourteen of the nineteen successful challengers for the House in 1978 exceeded the limit on PAC receipts that would have been imposed by the Obey-Railsback bill.[9] Thus, stingy limits on how much candidates could receive from corporate PACs and others might spread these contributions more evenly but not in sufficient amounts to do challengers much good, especially if such limits were coupled with limits on campaign spending.

On the other hand, relatively high limits on PAC receipts might shift contributions marginally from the powerful to the needy without handicapping challengers. In the 1986 elections for the House, for example, the top fifty recipients of PAC money received total contributions from all types of PACs ranging from $221,000 to $526,000. The list, which includes only one challenger and three open seats, reads like a who's who of House notables, especially on the Democratic side.[10] A generous limit on total PAC receipts—say double the $90,000 of Obey-Glickman-Leach—and no limits on campaign spending would force corporate PACs and others away from these magnets for contributions while not unduly restricting challengers' spending. Of course, providing assistance to challengers has never been high on Congress's agenda for campaign reform, so that these are hardly the kinds of limits that are likely to be enacted.

There was a time when talk of limits was a red flag to the PAC community, and in some quarters it still is. About the bills with limits currently before Congress Mick Stanton of the Chamber of Commerce complained that "once you sit down with these guys and start talking about whether this much (PAC money) is too much, it indicates your acquiescence to the point that there's something wrong about the dollars that make up that contribution. We don't believe there is.... We're taking a hard line approach. What we'd like to see happen is to increase the doggone limits."[11] Still, the opposition of many business PACs to restrictions of any sort has softened. Indeed, the National Association of Business Political Action Committees has itself proposed new regulations, including the restriction of PAC contributions to one election cycle and the prohibition of carryovers and redistribution to other candidates. The managers of other business PACs have gone so far as to support limits as a "kind of arms-control agreement in the fund raising area."[12]

The Evolution of Organizations and Tactics

That a growing number of business PACs would support formal or informal restrictions on campaign contributions is a symptom of the soberness that has come with the maturing of the PAC movement. There was an almost evangelical fervor in the initial wave of PAC formation among corporations and trade associations, for in the late 1970s PACs had come to be widely regarded as a panacea for the failings of public policies and the ills of American industries. A decade later some of this zeal has been lost along with the hopes for an imminent Republican millennium that some PACs may have harbored. The use of PACs to achieve specific advantages for firms has proven to be problematic as these sources of contributions have proliferated and members of Congress have adapted to the new campaign environment. Indeed, candidates' incessant demands for funds nave maae tne managers ot even the largest Washington PACs feel more like the hunted than the hunter. "The pressures are such on the Hill now," a staff member of the Public Affairs Council has observed, "that in a week's time you could give out all of your money. There have to be some lines drawn. We didn't want to see PAC money being wasted."[13] Many smaller PACs now find themselves as relatively insignificant players in this high-stakes game.[14]

A growing sense of the limits of their influence may be one reason for the slackened pace of PAC formation among corporations. The number of corporate PACs grew from 89 in 1974 to 433 in 1976 and 1,204 in 1980. Between 1980 and 1984, however, the number of these committees grew only to 1,682 and since then has remained flat. For a variety of reasons about 40 percent of the largest five hundred industrial corporations and 80 percent of the next largest five hundred have apparently elected not to form political action committees.[15] Moreover, some of those corporations and industry trade associations that had formed PACs have abandoned them, and other PACs have become dormant.[16]

None of this is to suggest that corporate PACs are an endangered species; the continued growth in their aggregate contributions in the 1980s is evidence to the contrary. What does appear likely is that corporate PACs will themselves adapt to the changing environment of politics and policy making in the United States. One such adaptation, which is already taking place, is the development of self-imposed rules to protect the PAC from the escalating demands of candidates.[17] An increasing number of corporate PACs, for example, now refuse as a matter of course to give contributions outside the election cycle, and some are giving only in the year of the election. Another growing practice is to provide endorsements but not money for safe incumbents so that contributions are given only to those candidates who need them. Bylaws prohibiting contributions to retire debt, contributions to both candidates in the same race, or gifts to the personal PACs of members of Congress have been adopted by some corporate PACs and are being considered by many others. Indeed, the Chamber of Commerce and other organizations now provide guidelines about how the PACs of their members can keep from squandering their funds.

The gridlock of money and interest groups on Capitol Hill, along with the New Federalism, has also expanded the field of vision of corporate PACs to include state politics. As states have become the locus of decision making for the implementation of regulation, corporations have become much more active in state races. As the director of public affairs for one chemical corporation put it:

> There's a great deal more emphasis on what happens at the state level.
> The trend is definitely toward more company involvement at that
> level. Foremost in our mind is fiscal management—taxes and spend-
> ing—which is a problem for all states. We have an interest in the
> candidate's position on environmental issues, the regulatory process,
> right-to-know legislation, hazardous waste management and energy.[18]

The rate of growth of PACs of all sorts in the states has been impressive. In
California, where state legislative contests may attract as much money as congressional races in other states, contributions from PACs increased by 39 percent between election cycles.[19] Similar increases have been reported in other
states, and in most of these states business and professional PACs have been the
fastest growing.[20] These increases in expenditures are likely to continue, and for
some businesses state and local PACs have become important elements in the
building of grass-roots political organizations.[21]

Indeed, the most interesting response to the arms race of campaign contributions may be more emphasis on the nonpecuniary functions of the PAC. Relatively few corporate PACs, after all, have the financial wherewithal to compete
nationally with other interests for influence in campaigns and policy making.
And we have seen that for many corporations the PAC may serve purposes
other than financial intermediation, including increasing the company's visibility, educating management employees, and building the organizational capacity
for grass-roots lobbying. These new forms of corporate political activity are as
significant as the more widely remarked campaign money of business,[22] and the
continued growth of countervailing powers in the election economy may make
these activities even more important.

There is evidence that in some cases the committee originally organized as a
simple conduit of money may be becoming "a political organization that functions midway between the party and the PAC. Its range of concerns will be
neither limited to a single issue nor fully comprehensive in its program, and its
electoral role will combine the activities and strategies of voter mobilization with
those of legislative influence."[23] To be sure, labor PACs and some ideological
PACs are closer to becoming "quasi-parties"[24] than business PACs are, and
restraint, refinement, and decentralization in their political giving are the likely
responses of most corporations to the changing political environment. Still, it
would be equally in error now to underestimate the capacity and willingness of
corporations to engage in political mobilization as it was to exaggerate it at the
beginning of the decade.

Business and Politics in the Post-Reagan Era

In the final analysis the means of corporate political mobilization are less
important than its ends. The corporate PAC movement reflects a tension
between pragmatism and partisanship in the dealings of business with the state, a

tension born of the unique development of business–government relations in the United States. It reflects as well a tension between the individual and collective interests of firms. Depending on the eye of the beholder, therefore, corporate PACs can be at once unified and fragmented, ideological and pragmatic, partisan and nonpartisan. Our goal has been to illuminate these tensions and, more importantly, to identify the sources of diversity and change among PACs.

This inquiry has led us in several directions: to the internal lives of these new styles of political organization and to their geographic roots in the center or periphery of politics, to the variegated regulatory relationships between business and government, to the expanding networks among PACs and between them and other political actors. Ultimately, it leads to the very wellsprings of contemporary American politics, for PACs are in many respects the product of the evolving structures of institutions and campaigning in the United States. Above all perhaps, the system of PACs is a product of the individualism of the contemporary Congress. Members of Congress get to the institution as individuals, and whether it is by dividing policy turf as in the 1970s or by the rule of all by all through collegial decision making in the 1980s, they govern as individuals.[25] This being the case, it is little wonder that individual candidates remain the relevant units of campaign politics, including finances.

It was the apparent rise of partisanship in the midst of this candidate-centered politics that made the temporary alliance between PACs and parties at the beginning of this decade so intriguing. This alliance between the PACs of business and others with the Republican party was made possible in part by the Republican National Committee's then-substantial advantage in organization and technology, a gap that will inevitably be closed by counteroffensives of the Democrats. In the long run, therefore, it is not simply technology that will determine the relationship between the PACs and the parties. Instead political action committees will be both a response to and a catalyst for changes in the party coalitions. Nowhere is this clearer than in the Sunbelt, where the PACs of business have been in the vanguard of a secular realignment toward the Republican party.[26]

More than students of American party politics have acknowledged, realignments are matters not simply of elections but of policy, of "the way in which political leaders, the policies they formulate, and the institutions they create also reshape political life, turning it in new directions that the electorate then endorses."[27] Indeed, it was the perception of a common threat from the course of public policy in the 1970s that galvanized business interests.[28] And it was the coincidence of this mobilization with similar policy appeals to the electorate by Ronald Reagan that helped not only to shift, perhaps only temporarily, the party coalitions but also to alter the political agenda itself.

What comes after success? By some accounts, the transformation of business's once-controversial agenda into more or less settled policy means a return to politics as usual, in which the pursuit of individual competitive advantage once again becomes more important than collective action.[29] The 1984 election can certainly be read this way. Yet in a politics as atomistic as ours has become there is a risk in regarding anything as settled policy. Indeed, the political agenda for the post-Reagan era seems anything but settled. On the political horizon are a host of issues—plant-closing legislation, restrictions on mergers, parental leaves for employees, and comparable pay for comparable work—that are different in kind but no less threatening to the autonomy of the corporation than the social regulations of the 1970s. In these matters business could well find itself in conflict with other powerful social groups in the years ahead.

On more basic issues—the federal budget, taxation, international trade, manpower, and social welfare policy—consensus has been elusive, and the public interest has fallen victim to the sum of individual interests, including those within the business community. In the last decade American business has been the subject of encomiums, which have identified the public interest with business interests, as well as indictments decrying this identification as false. On these and a host of other difficult issues, the challenge for business will be to demonstrate that its growing political power is in fact harnessed to the public good.

Notes

1. Frank J. Sorauf, "Political Parties and Political Action Committees: Two Life Cycles," *Arizona Law Review* 22, no. 2 (1980), p. 463.

2. On these developments see Thomas R. Kiley, "PACing the Burger Court: The Corporate Right to Speak and the Public Right to Hear After *First National Bank v. Bellotti*," *Arizona Law Review* 22, no. 2 (1980), pp. 373–426; Richard Smolka, "The Campaign Law in the Courts," in Michael J. Malbin, ed., *Money and Politics in the United States* (Chatham, NJ: Chatham House, 1984), pp. 214–31; Michael J. Malbin, "Introduction," in Malbin, ed., *Money and Politics in the United States*, pp. 1–10; Jan W. Baran, "The Federal Election Commission: A Guide for Corporate Counsel," *Arizona Law Review* 22, no. 2 (1980), pp. 519–38.

3. Henry C. Kenski, "Running With And From The PAC," *Arizona Law Review* 22, no. 2 (1980), pp. 627–52; Herbert E. Alexander, "The Obey-Railsback Bill: Its Genesis and Early History," *Arizona Law Review* 22, no. 2 (1980), pp. 653–66.

4. William J. Keefe, *Congress and the American People*, 3d ed. (Englewood Cliffs, NJ: Prentice-Hall, 1988), p. 64.

5. This bill, authored by representatives David Obey, Dan Glickman, and Jim Leach and cosponsored by seventy-two others, is analyzed in detail in Michael J. Malbin, "Looking Back at the Future of Campaign Finance Reform: Interest Groups and American Elections," in Malbin, ed., *Money and Politics in the United States*, pp. 232–76.

6. Republicans have been more inclined to take different routes to reform. For example, the Laxalt-Frenzel bill of 1983 would have greatly expanded the role of political parties by doing away with restrictions on coordinated spending. Most recently Senator Mitch McConnell has proposed doing away with all political action committees and allowing contributions only by individuals and political parties. The advantage these proposals would give to Republicans, at least in the short term, makes them unlikely candidates for enactment.

7. Malbin, "Looking Back at the Future of Campaign Finance Reform," p. 270.

8. Theodore J. Eismeier and Philip H. Pollock III, "An Organizational Analysis of Political Action Committees," *Political Behavior* 7, no. 2 (1985), pp. 192–216; Anne B. Matasar, *Corporate PACs and Federal Campaign Financing Laws* (Westport, CT: Quorum Books, 1986), ch. 6.

9. Carroll A. Campbell, Jr., "In Response to Obey-Railsback," *Arizona Law Review* 22, no. 2 (1980), pp. 672–74.

10. Consider this sample of Democratic notables from the list: Jim Wright, $432,000; William Gray, $401,000; Richard Gephardt, $347,000; Thomas Foley, $327,000; John Dingell, $295,000; Charles Rangel, $280,000; Claude Pepper, $273,000; Tony Coelho, $268,000. Republican notables included Robert Michel, $417,000, and Jack Kemp, $256,000. *Federal Election Commission Release* (October 31, 1986).

11. Quoted in Tom Watson, "Business PACs Wary of Campaign Finance Bill," *CQ Weekly Reports* (April 25, 1987), pp. 782–84.

12. Burt Solomon, "When Fat Cats Cry Foul: Last Fall's Record Round of Money-Grubbing Left Business Lobbyists Annoyed with the Fund-Raising System and Unsure They Are Getting Their Money's Worth," *National Journal* 19 (February 21, 1987), p. 422.

13. Quoted in Richard L. Berke, "PACs Devise Bylaws to Limit Their Giving," *New York Times* (October 26, 1987), p. A16.

14. Steve Coll, "Political PAC Men: Small-Business Money Is Too Meager to Compete for Power and Influence in Washington," *Inc.* 7 (August 1985), p. 22; Kevin Farrell, "Do Small Business PACs Pay?" *Venture* 1, no. 1 (April 1983), pp. 98–100.

15. Matasar, *Corporate PACs and Federal Campaign Financing Laws*, ch. 3. In Matasar's survey the most commonly cited reasons for not having a PAC were lack of need, a belief that political activity was inappropriate because of the nature of the business, fear of alienating employees and shareholders, and disenchantment with PACs.

16. See, for example, "Why a PAC Decided to Pack It In," *Nation's Business* 71 (December 1983), p. 17.

17. We draw here on the descriptions of these new rules of restraint in Solomon, "When Fat Cats Cry Foul," and Berke, "PACs Devise Bylaws to Limit Their Giving."

18. "Where the Political Action Is," *Chemical Business* (January 10, 1983), p. 5. See also Timothy D. Schellhardt, "Corporate PACs Turning Attention to States as Deregulation Gains," *Wall Street Journal* (October 28, 1982), p. 33.

19. "Where the Political Action Is," p. 5.

20. Ruth S. Jones, "Financing State Elections," in Malbin, ed., *Money and Politics in the United States*, pp. 172–213.

21. Bernadette A. Budde, "The Practical Role of Corporate PACs in the Political Process," *Arizona Law Review* 22, no. 2 (1980), p. 567.

22. This argument is made persuasively in Malbin, "Looking Back at the Future of Campaign Finance Reform."

23. Sorauf, "Political Parties and Political Action Committees: Two Life Cycles," p. 458.

24. Sorauf, "Political Action Committees in American Politics: An Overview," in *What Price PACs?* (New York: Twentieth Century Fund, 1984), pp. 76–79.

25. Steven S. Smith, "New Patterns of Decisionmaking in Congress," in John E. Chubb and Paul E. Peterson, eds., *The New Direction in American Politics* (Washington, DC: The Brookings Institution, 1985), pp. 203–34.

26. For evidence on this point see Eismeier and Pollock, "The Geopolitics of PACs," paper delivered at the annual meeting of the Midwest Political Science Association, Chicago, April 18–20, 1985.

27. John E. Chubb and Paul E. Peterson, "Realignment and Institutionalization," in Chubb and Peterson, eds., *The New Direction in American Politics*, p. 3.

28. David Vogel, "The Power of Business in America: A Reappraisal," *British Journal of Political Science* 13, no. 1 (January 1983), pp. 19–43.

29. Vogel, "The Study of Social Issues in Management: A Critical Appraisal," *California Management Review* 28, no. 1 (Winter 1986), pp. 142–51.

Selected Bibliography

Adamany, David. "PACs and the Democratic Financing of Politics." *Arizona Law Review* 22, no. 2 (1980): 569–602.

———. "Political Parties in the 1980's." In *Money and Politics in the United States*, ed. Michael J. Malbin, pp. 70–121. Chatham, NJ: Chatham House, 1984.

Alexander, Herbert E. "The Obey-Railsback Bill: Its Genesis and Early History." *Arizona Law Review* 22, no. 2 (1980): 653–56.

Aplin, John C., and W. Harvey Hegarty. "Political Influence: Strategies Employed by Organizations to Impact Legislation in Business and Economic Matters." *Academy of Management Review* 23, no. 3 (September 1980): 438–50.

"Are PACs Revolutionizing Politics?" *Chemical Business* (August 23, 1982): 27–29.

"Arms Concerns Double Contributions." *New York Times* (April 9, 1985): 40.

Baran, Jan W. "The Federal Election Commission: A Guide for Corporate Counsel." *Arizona Law Review* 22, no. 2 (1980): 519–38.

Bardach, Eugene, and Robert A. Kagan. *Going By the Book*. Philadelphia, PA: Temple University Press, 1982.

———, eds. *Social Regulation: Strategies for Reform*. San Francisco, CA: Institute for Contemporary Studies, 1982.

Bauer, Raymond, Ithiel De Sola Pool, and Lewis Anthony Dexter. *American Business and Public Policy*. New York: Atherton Press, 1964.

Baysinger, Barry D. "Domain Maintenance as an Objective of Business Political Activity: An Expanded Typology." *Academy of Management Review* 9, no. 2 (April 1984): 248–58.

Berke, Richard L. "PACs Devise Bylaws to Limit Their Giving." *New York Times* (October 26, 1987): 16.

Berry, Jeffrey M. *Lobbying for the People*. Princeton, NJ: Princeton University Press, 1977.

Bretton, Henry. *The Power of Money*. Albany, NY: State University of New York Press, 1980.

Breyer, Stephen. *Regulation and Its Reform*. Cambridge: Harvard University Press, 1982.

Brown, Kirk F. "National Financing of Local Elections." Paper delivered at the annual meeting of the American Political Science Association, Chicago, September 3–6, 1987.

Budde, Bernadette A. "The Practical Role of Corporate PACs in the Political Process." *Arizona Law Review* 22, no. 2 (1980): 555–68.

Burris, Val. "The Political Partisanship of American Business: A Study of Corporate Political Action Committees." *American Sociological Review* 52, no. 6 (December 1987): 732–44.

"Business 'Double Dips' for Candidates." *Business Week* (August 16, 1982): 113.

Campbell, Carroll A., Jr. "In Response to Obey-Railsback." *Arizona Law Review* 22, no. 2 (1980): 672–74.

Cavanagh, Thomas E., and James L. Sundquist. "The New Two Party System." In *The New Direction in American Politics*, ed. John E. Chubb and Paul E. Peterson, pp. 35–68. Washington, DC: The Brookings Institution, 1985.

Chandler, Alfred D., Jr. "Government Versus Business: An American Phenomenon." In *Business and Public Policy*, ed. John T. Dunlop, pp. 1–11. Cambridge: Harvard University Press, 1980.

Chappell, Henry W., Jr. "Campaign Contributions and Congressional Voting: A Simultaneous Probit-Tobit Model." *Review of Economics and Statistics* 64 (February 1982): 77–83.

Chubb, John E., and Paul E. Peterson. "Realignment and Institutionalization." In *The New Direction in American Politics*, ed. John E. Chubb and Paul E. Peterson, pp. 1–32. Washington, DC: The Brookings Institution, 1985.

Clark, Timothy B. "How One Company Lives with Government Regulation." *National Journal* (May 12, 1979): 772–79.

Clawson, Dan, Alan Neustadtl, and James Bearden. "The Logic of Business Unity: Corporate Contributions in the 1980 Congressional Elections." *American Sociological Review* 51, no. 6 (December 1986): 797–811.

Close, Arthur, ed. *Washington Representatives: Who Does What for Whom in the Nation's Capital?* Washington, DC: Columbia Press, 1984.

Coll, Steve. "Political PAC Men: Small-Business Money Is Too Meager to Compete for Power and Influence in Washington." *Inc.* 7 (August 1985): 22.

Dickson, Douglas N. "CORPACS: The Business of Political Action Committees." *Across the Board* 18 (November 1981): 13–22.

Drew, Elizabeth. *Politics and Money*. New York: Macmillan, 1983.

Dye, Thomas. "Oligarchic Tendencies in National Policymaking: The Role of Private Policy-Planning Organizations." *Journal of Politics* 40, no. 2 (May 1978): 309–31.

Edsall, Thomas B. "Business is Ambivalent about Worth of PACs." *Washington Post* (March 27, 1986): A19.

————. "If You've Got the Dime, Coelho's Got the Ear." *Washington Post National Weekly Edition* (December 23, 1985): 14.

————. *The New Politics of Inequality*. New York: W. W. Norton and Co., 1984.

Eismeier, Theodore J., and Philip H. Pollock III. "The Retreat from Partisanship: Why the Dog Didn't Bark in 1984." In *Business Strategy and Public Policy*, ed. Alfred A. Marcus, Allen M. Kaufman, and David R. Beam, pp. 137–50. Westport, CT: Quorum Books, 1987.

————. "Politics and Markets: Corporate Money in American National Elections." *British Journal of Political Science* 16, no. 3 (July 1986): 187–209.

_____. "A Tale of Two Elections: PAC Money in 1980 and 1984." *Corruption and Reform* 1 (1986): 189–207.

_____. "Strategy and Choice in Congressional Elections: The Role of Political Action Committees." *American Journal of Political Science* 30, no. 1 (February 1986): 197–213.

_____. "An Organizational Analysis of Political Action Committees." *Political Behavior* 7, no. 2 (1985): 192–216.

_____. "The Geopolitics of PACs." Paper delivered at the annual meeting of the Midwest Political Science Association, Chicago, April 18–20, 1985.

_____. "Political Action Committees: Varieties of Organization and Strategy." In *Money and Politics in the United States*, ed. Michael J. Malbin, pp. 122–41. Chatham, NJ: Chatham House, 1984.

Elliott, Lee Ann. "Political Action Committees: Precincts of the 1980's." *Arizona Law Review* 22, no. 2 (1980): 539–54.

Epstein, Edwin M. "PACs and the Modern Political Process." In *The Impact of the Modern Corporation*, ed. Betty Bock, Harvey J. Goldschmid, Ira M. Millstein, and F. M. Scherer, pp. 399–496. New York: Columbia University Press, 1984.

_____. "The PAC Phenomenon: An Overview-Introduction." *Arizona Law Review* 22, no. 2 (1980): 355–72.

_____. *The Corporation in American Politics*. Englewood Cliffs, NJ: Prentice-Hall, 1969.

Etzioni, Amitai. *Capital Corruption*. New York: Harcourt Brace Jovanovich, 1984.

Farney, Dennis. "A Liberal Congressman Turns Conservative: Did PACs Do It?" *Wall Street Journal* (July 29, 1982): 1.

Farrell, Kevin. "Do Small Business PACs Pay?" *Venture* 1, no. 1 (April 1983): 98–100.

Fenno, Richard F. "If, As Ralph Nader Says, Congress is 'The Broken Branch,' How Come We Love Our Congressmen So Much?" In *Congress in Change*, ed. Norman J. Ornstein, pp. 277–87. New York: Praeger, 1975.

Ferguson, Thomas, and Joel Rogers. "The Reagan Victory: Corporate Coalitions in the 1980 Campaign." In *The Hidden Election*, ed. Thomas Ferguson and Joel Rogers, pp. 3–64. New York: Pantheon Books, 1981.

Fialka, John J., and Tim Carrington. "The Money Tree: Wall Street's Firms Broaden Gift Lists for Congress Members." *Wall Street Journal* (October 17, 1983): 1.

"Firms That Manage Business Associations." *D&B Reports* 34 (November/December 1986): 54–55.

Gais, Thomas L., Mark A. Peterson, and Jack L. Walker. "Interest Groups, Iron Triangles, and Representative Institutions in American National Government." *British Journal of Political Science* 14, no. 2 (April 1984): 161–86.

Galambos, Louis. *The Public Image of Big Business in America, 1880–1940*. Baltimore, MD: The Johns Hopkins University Press, 1975.

Glen, Maxwell. "At the Wire, Corporate PACs Come Through for the GOP." *National Journal* (February 3, 1979): 174.

Goldenberg, Edie N., and Michael W. Traugott. *Campaigning for Congress*. Washington, DC: Congressional Quarterly Press, 1984.

Gopoian, David J. "What Makes PACs Tick? An Analysis of the Allocation Patterns of Economic Interest Groups." *American Journal of Political Science* 28 (May 1984): 259–81.

Gormley, William T., Jr. *The Politics of Public Utility Regulation*. Pittsburgh, PA: University of Pittsburgh Press, 1983.

Grier, Kevin B., and Michael C. Munger. "The Impact of Legislator Attributes on Interest-Group Campaign Contributions." *Journal of Labor Research* 7, no. 4 (Fall 1986): 349–64.

Handler, Edward, and John R. Mulkern. *Business in Politics: Campaign Strategies of Corporate Political Action Committees.* Lexington, MA: Lexington Books, 1982.

Harris, Richard A. "Politicized Management: Business' Response to the New Social Regulation." Paper delivered at the annual meeting of the American Political Science Association, New Orleans, August 29–September 1, 1985.

Hayes, Michael T. "The New Group Universe." In *Interest Group Politics*, 2d ed., ed. Allan J. Cigler and Burdett A. Loomis, pp. 133–45. Washington, DC: Congressional Quarterly Press, 1986.

————. *Lobbyists and Legislators*. New Brunswick, NJ: Rutgers University Press, 1981.

Heclo, Hugh, and Rudolph G. Penner. "Fiscal and Political Strategy in the Reagan Administration." In *The Reagan Presidency*, ed. Fred I. Greenstein, pp. 21–47. Baltimore, MD: The Johns Hopkins University Press, 1983.

Hessen, Robert, ed. *Does Big Business Rule America?* Washington, DC: Ethics and Public Policy Center, 1981.

Hirschman, Albert O. *Exit, Voice, and Loyalty*. Cambridge: Harvard University Press, 1970.

Hunt, Albert R. "National Politics and the 1982 Campaign." In *The American Elections of 1982*, ed. Thomas E. Mann and Norman J. Ornstein, pp. 1–43. Washington, DC: American Enterprise Institute, 1983.

Jackson, Brooks. "Ways and Means Measure Puts Bigger Tax Bites on Some of the Most Prolific Campaign Donors." *Wall Street Journal* (December 11, 1985): 64.

————. "Insurance Industry Boosts Political Contributions as Congress Takes Up Cherished Tax Preferences." *Wall Street Journal* (October 10, 1985): 64.

————. "Business Money Flows to Representative Gore." *Wall Street Journal* (February 15, 1984): 50.

Jacobson, Gary C. *The Politics of Congressional Elections*. Boston: Little, Brown, 1987.

————. "Congress: Politics After a Landslide Without Coattails." In *The Elections of 1984*, ed. Michael Nelson, pp. 215–38. Washington, DC: Congressional Quarterly Press, 1985.

————. "The Republican Advantage in Campaign Finance." In *The New Direction in American Politics*, ed. John E. Chubb and Paul E. Peterson, pp. 143–74. Washington, DC: The Brookings Institution, 1985.

————. "Money in the 1980 and 1982 Congressional Elections." In *Money and Politics in the United States*, ed. Michael J. Malbin, pp. 38–69. Chatham, NJ: Chatham House, 1984.

Jacobson, Gary C., and Samuel J. Kernell. *Strategy and Choice in Congressional Elections*. New Haven, CT: Yale University Press, 1981.

Johnson, Linda L. "The Impact of Real Estate Political Action Committees on Congressional Voting and Elections." *AREUEA Journal* 11, no. 4 (Winter 1983): 462–75.

Jones, Ruth S. "Financing State Elections." In *Money and Politics in the United States*, ed. Michael J. Malbin, pp. 172–213. Chatham, NJ: Chatham House, 1984.

Joseph, Lawrence B. "Corporate Political Power and Liberal Democratic Theory." *Polity* 15, no. 2 (Winter 1982): 246–67.

Kau, James B., and Paul H. Rubin. *Congressmen, Constituents, and Contributors*. Boston: Martinus Nijhoff, 1982.

Keefe, William J. *Congress and the American People*, 3d ed. Englewood Cliffs, NJ: Prentice-Hall, 1988.

Keim, Gerald. "Corporate Grassroots Programs in the 1980's." *California Management Review* 28, no. 1 (Fall 1985): 110–23.

Keim, Gerald D., Carl P. Zeithami, and Barry D. Baysinger. "New Directions for Corporate Political Strategy." *Sloan Management Review* 25 (Spring 1984): 53–62.

Kelman, Steven. *Regulating America, Regulating Sweden: A Comparative Study of Occupational Safety and Health Policy*. Cambridge, MA: The MIT Press, 1981.

Kenski, Henry C. "Running With And From The PAC." *Arizona Law Review* 22, no. 2 (1980): 627–52.

Kiley, Thomas R. "PACing the Burger Court: The Corporate Right to Speak and the Public Right to Hear After *First National Bank v. Bellotti*." *Arizona Law Review* 22, no. 2 (1980): 373–426.

Kolko, Gabriel. *The Triumph of Conservatism*. Chicago: Quadrangle, 1967.

Krim, Arthur B. "Comments and Dissents." In *What Price PACs?*, pp. 13–17. New York: Twentieth Century Fund, 1984.

Latus, Margaret Ann. "Assessing Ideological PACs: From Outrage to Understanding." In *Money and Politics in the United States*, ed. Michael J. Malbin, pp. 142–71. Chatham, NJ: Chatham House, 1984.

Lave, Lester B. *The Strategy of Social Regulation: Decision Frameworks for Policy*. Washington, DC: The Brookings Institution, 1981.

Leone, Robert A. *Who Profits?* New York: Basic Books, 1986.

Lilley, William, and James C. Miller III. "The New Social Regulation." *The Public Interest* 47 (Spring 1977): 49–61.

Lindblom, Charles E. *Politics and Markets*. New York: Basic Books, 1977.

Lipset, Seymour Martin, Martin Trow, and James Coleman. *Union Democracy*. Garden City, NY: Anchor Books, 1956.

Litan, Robert E., and William D. Nordhaus. *Reforming Federal Regulation*. New Haven, CT: Yale University Press, 1983.

Lowi, Theodore J. *The End of Liberalism*. New York: W. W. Norton and Co., 1969.

MacAvoy, Paul W. *The Regulated Industries and the Economy*. New York: W. W. Norton and Co., 1979.

McCaw, Thomas K. "Business and Government: The Origins of the Adversary Relationship." *California Management Review* 26, no. 2 (Winter 1984): 33–52.

————. "Regulation in America: A Historical Overview." *California Management Review* 27, no. 1 (Fall 1984): 116–24.

McConnell, Grant. *Private Power and American Democracy*. New York: Alfred A. Knopf, 1966.

McFarland, Andrew S. "Interest Groups and Theories of Power in America." *British Journal of Political Science* 17, no. 2 (April 1987): 129–47.

————. *Public Interest Lobbies*. Washington, DC: American Enterprise Institute for Public Policy Research, 1976.

Maitland, Ian. "Self-Defeating Lobbying: How More Is Buying Less in Washington." *Journal of Business Strategy* 7 (Fall 1986): 67–74.

Malbin, Michael J. "Looking Back at the Future of Campaign Finance Reform: Interest Groups in American Elections." In *Money and Politics in the United*

States, ed. Michael J. Malbin, pp. 232–76. Chatham, NJ: Chatham House, 1984.

————. "Campaign Financing and the 'Special Interests.'" *The Public Interest* 56 (December 1979): 21–42.

Manley, John. "Neopluralism: A Class Analysis of Pluralism I and Pluralism II." *American Political Science Review* 77, no. 2 (June 1983): 368–83.

Maraniss, David. "PAC Heaven: Commerce Committee Members Roll Up Contributions." *Washington Post* (August 21, 1983): A1.

Marcus, Alfred A. *The Adversary Economy*. Westport, CT: Quorum Books, 1984.

Margolis, Howard. *Selfishness, Altruism, and Rationality*. Chicago: University of Chicago Press, 1982.

Markowitz, Steven. "Ethical Rules for Corporate PAC-Men." *Business and Society Review* (Summer, 1984): 21–25.

Masters, Marick F., and Gerald D. Keim. "Variation on Corporate PAC and Lobbying Activity: An Organizational and Environmental Analysis." In *Research in Corporate Social Performance and Policy*, vol 8., pp. 249–71. Greenwich, CT: JAI Press, 1986.

————. "Determinants of PAC Participation Among Large Corporations." *Journal of Politics* 47, no. 4 (November 1985): 1158–73.

Matasar, Ann B. *Corporate PACs and Federal Campaign Financing Laws*. Westport, CT: Quorum Books, 1986.

Meier, Kenneth J. *Regulation: Politics, Bureaucracy, and Economics*. New York: St. Martin's Press, 1985.

Miller, Arthur Selwyn. *The Modern Corporate State*. Westport, CT: Greenwood Press, 1976.

Miller, W. H. "Why Firms Shun Political Drumbeating." *Industry Week* 206 (September 29, 1980): 17–19.

Moe, Terry M. *The Organization of Interests*. Chicago: University of Chicago Press, 1980.

Mosher, Lawrence. "Big Steel Says It Can't Afford to Make the Nation's Air Pure." *National Journal* (July 5, 1980): 1088–92.

Olson, Mancur, Jr. *The Logic of Collective Action*. Cambridge: Harvard University Press, 1965.

Overacker, Louise. *Money in Elections*. New York: Macmillan, 1932.

Parkinson, Hank. "Is the PAC Parade Passing You By?" *Association Management* 31 (May 1979): 29–32.

Perrow, Charles. "Members as Resources in Voluntary Associations." In *Organizations and Clients*, ed. Walter R. Rosengren, pp. 93–116. Columbus, OH: Charles E. Merrill, 1970.

Pertschuck, Michael. *The Revolt Against Regulation*. Berkeley: University of California Press, 1982.

Pires, Mary Ann. "Fertile Fields: The Realization that Politics Starts at Home Has Led to a Harvest of Corporate Grass-Roots Programs." *Public Relations Journal* 42 (November 1986): 36–41.

Plotkin, Sidney. "Corporate Power and Political Resistance: The Case of the Energy Mobilization Board." *Polity* 18, no. 1 (Fall 1985): 115–37.

Post, James E., Edwin A. Murray, Jr., Robert B. Dickie, and John F. Mahon. "Managing Public Affairs: The Public Affairs Function." *California Management Review* 26, no. 1 (Fall 1983): 135–50.

Ranney, Austin. *Channels of Power*. New York: Basic Books, 1983.

Reichley, A. James. "The Rise of National Parties." In *The New Direction in American Politics*, ed. John E. Chubb and Paul E. Peterson, pp. 175–202. Washington, DC: The Brookings Institution, 1985.

Sabato, Larry J. *PAC Power*. New York: W. W. Norton and Co., 1985.

Salisbury, Robert H. "Business and Government in America: Ordinary Clout and Contingent Privilege." Paper delivered at the annual meeting of the Midwest Political Science Association, Chicago, April 18–20, 1985.

————. "Interest Representation: The Dominance of Institutions." *American Political Science Review* 78, no. 1 (March 1984): 64–76.

————. "An Exchange Theory of Interest Groups." *Midwest Journal of Political Science* 13, no. 1 (February 1969): 1–32.

Saltzman, Gregory M. "Congressional Voting on Labor Issues: The Role of PACs." *Industrial and Labor Relations Review* 40, no. 2 (January 1987): 163–79.

Saperstein, Saundra. "Local, Small Businesses Forming Own PAC Groups." *Washington Post* (October 30, 1982): A7.

Schatz, Willie. "The Name of the Game Is Now Political Action: Long a 'Sleeping Giant' the Computer Industry Is Now Waking Up to the Importance of PACs." *Datamation* 33 (January 1, 1987): 41–48.

Schellhardt, Timothy D. "Corporate PACs Turning Attention to States as Deregulation Gains." *Wall Street Journal* (October 28, 1982): 33.

Schelling, Thomas. *Micromotives and Macrobehavior*. New York: W. W. Norton and Co., 1978.

Schlozman, Kay. "What Accent the Heavenly Chorus? Political Equality and the American Pressure System." *Journal of Politics* 46, no. 4 (November 1984): 1006–32.

Schlozman, Kay L., and John T. Tierney. *Organized Interests and American Democracy*. New York: Harper and Row, 1986.

Schultze, Charles L. *The Public Use of Private Interest*. Washington, DC: The Brookings Institution, 1977.

Sethi, S. Prakash. "Corporate Political Activism." *California Management Review* 24, no. 3 (Spring 1982): 32–42.

Shipper, Frank, and Marianne M. Jennings. *Business Strategy for the Political Arena*. Westport, CT: Quorum Books, 1984.

Silberman, Jonathan I., and Gary C. Durden. "Determining Legislative Preferences on the Minimum Wage: An Economic Approach." *Journal of Political Economy* 84, No. 2 (April, 1976): 317–29.

Skowronek, Stephen. *Building a New American State*. Cambridge: Cambridge University Press, 1982.

Smith, Steven S. "New Patterns of Decisionmaking in Congress." In *The New Direction in American Politics*, ed. John E. Chubb and Paul E. Peterson, pp. 203–34. Washington, DC: The Brookings Institution, 1985.

Smolka, Richard. "The Campaign Law in the Courts." In *Money and Politics in the United States*, ed. Michael J. Malbin, pp. 214–31. Chatham, NJ: Chatham House, 1984.

Solomon, Burt. "When Fat Cats Cry Foul: Last Fall's Record Round of Money-Grubbing Left Business Lobbyists Annoyed with the Fund-Raising System and Unsure They Are Getting Their Money's Worth." *National Journal* 19 (February 21, 1987): 418–22.

Sorauf, Frank J. "Campaign Money and the Press: Three Soundings." *Political Science Quarterly* 102, no. 1 (Spring 1987): 25–42.

_____. "Varieties of Experience: Campaign Finance in the House and Senate." In *Elections in America*, ed. Kay Lehman Schlozman, pp. 197–218. Boston: Allen and Unwin, 1987.

_____. "Who's in Charge? Accountability in Political Action Committees." *Political Science Quarterly* 99, no. 4 (Winter 1984–1985): 591–614.

_____. "Political Action Committees in American Politics: An Overview." In *What Price PACs?*, pp. 27–137. New York: Twentieth Century Fund, 1984.

_____. "Political Parties and Political Action Committees: Two Life Cycles." *Arizona Law Review* 22, no. 2 (1980): 445–64.

"Spending Smarter on Political Candidates." *Business Week* (November 3, 1980): 42.

Stewart, Robert W., and Tracy Wood. "Political Giving: Corporate Contributions Buy Access." *Los Angeles Times* (October 26, 1986): 1.

Stigler, George. "The Theory of Economic Regulation." *Bell Journal of Economics and Management* 2, no. 1 (Spring 1971): 1–21.

Sutton, Francis X., Seymour E. Harris, Carl Kaysen, and James Tobin. *The American Business Creed*. Cambridge: Harvard University Press, 1956.

Thayer, George. *Who Shakes the Money Tree*. New York: Simon and Schuster, 1973.

Thoma, George A. "The Behavior of Corporate Action Committees." *Business and Society* 22 (Spring 1983): 55–58.

Tolchin, Susan J., and Martin Tolchin. *Dismantling America*. Boston: Houghton Mifflin, 1983.

Truman, David B. *The Governmental Process*, 2d ed. New York: Alfred A. Knopf, 1971.

Useem, Michael. "The Rise of the Political Manager." *Sloan Management Review* 27 (Fall 1985): 15–26.

_____. *The Inner Circle*. Oxford: Oxford University Press, 1984.

Vogel, David. "The New Political Science of Corporate Power." *The Public Interest* 87 (Spring 1987): 63–79.

_____. *National Styles of Regulation: Environmental Policy in Great Britain and the United States*. Ithaca, NY: Cornell University Press, 1986.

_____. "The Study of Social Issues in Management: A Critical Appraisal." *California Management Review* 28, no. 1 (Winter 1986): 142–51.

_____. "The Power of Business in the United States: A Reappraisal." *British Journal of Political Science* 13, no. 1 (January 1983): 19–43.

_____. "The 'New' Social Regulation in Historical and Comparative Perspective." In *Regulation in Perspective*, ed. Thomas K. McCaw, pp. 155–86. Cambridge: Harvard University Press, 1981.

_____. "Why Businessmen Distrust Their State: The Political Consciousness of American Corporate Executives." *British Journal of Political Science* 8, no. 1 (January 1978): 45–78.

Walker, Jack L. "The Origins and Maintenance of Interest Groups in America." *American Political Science Review* 77, no. 2 (June 1983): 390–406.

Watson, Tom. "Business PACs Wary of Campaign Finance Bill." *CQ Weekly Reports* (April 25, 1987): 782–84.

_____. "Oil's Campaign Capital Running Dry." *CQ Weekly Reports* (May 17, 1986): 1109–12.

Weaver, Paul C. "Regulation, Social Policy, and Class Conflict." *The Public Interest* 50 (Winter 1978): 45–63.

Weinberger, Marvin, and David V. Greevy. *The PAC Directory*. Cambridge, MA: Ballinger, 1982.

Weinstein, James. *The Corporate Ideal in the Liberal State: 1900–1918*. Boston, MA: Beacon Press, 1968.

Welch, W. P. "Money and Votes: A Simultaneous Equation Model." *Public Choice* 36, no. 3 (1981): 209–34.

Wertheimer, Fred. "The PAC Phenomenon in American Politics." *Arizona Law Review* 22, no. 2 (1980): 603–26.

"Where the Political Action Is." *Chemical Business* (January 10, 1983): 5.

White, Lawrence J. *Reforming Regulation: Processes and Problems*. Englewood Cliffs, NJ: Prentice-Hall, 1981.

"Why a PAC Decided to Pack It In." *Nation's Business* 71 (December, 1983): 17.

Wiebe, Robert H. *The Search for Order*. New York: Hill and Wang. 1967.

_____. *Businessmen and Reform*. Cambridge: Harvard University Press, 1962.

Wilson, James Q. "Democracy and the Corporation." In *Does Big Business Rule America?*, ed. Robert Hessen, pp. 35–39. Washington, DC: Ethics and Public Policy Center, 1981.

_____. *The Politics of Regulation*. New York: Basic Books, 1980.

_____. *Political Organizations*. New York: Basic Books, 1973.

Wood, Donna. *Strategic Uses of Public Policy: Business and Government in the Progressive Era*. Boston: Pitman, 1985.

Wright, John R. "PACs, Contributions, and Roll Calls: An Organizational Perspective." *American Political Science Review* 79, no. 2 (June 1985): 400–14.

Yoffie, David B., and Sigrid Bergenstein. "Creating Political Advantage: The Rise of the Corporate Political Entrepreneur." *California Management Review* 28, no. 1 (Fall 1985): 124–39.

Zardkoohi, Asghar. "On the Political Participation of the Firm in the Electoral Process." *Southern Economic Journal* 51 (January 1985): 804–18.

Zuckerman, Edward. *Almanac of Federal PACs, 1986*. Washington, DC: Amward Publications, 1986.

Index

About the Authors

THEODORE J. EISMEIER is Associate Professor of Government at Hamilton College. He is the coeditor of *Public Policy and Public Choice*, and his articles on American politics and public policy have appeared in the *Journal of Policy Analysis and Management*, *Americal Journal of Political Science*, *Political Behavior*, *Polity*, and in a number of edited volumes.

PHILIP H. POLLOCK III is Associate Professor of Political Science at the University of Central Florida. His recent publications include articles in the *British Journal of Political Science*, *American Journal of Political Science*, and *Western Political Quarterly*, as well as contributions to edited volumes.